One More Bridge to Cross

One More Bridge to Cross

Lowering the Cost of War

Illustrated

H. John Poole

Foreword by
William S. Lind

**Posterity
Press**

Published by Posterity Press
P.O. Box 5360, Emerald Isle, NC 28594

Cataloging-in-Publication Data

Poole, H.J., 1943-
One more bridge to cross.
    Includes bibliography and index.
    1. Infantry. 2. Infantry tactics. 3. Firepower.
    4. Military history. 5. Military art and science.
    6. Military education. 7. United States Marine Corps.
I. Title.   ISBN 0-9638695-3-1   1999   356'.1
Library of Congress Catalog Card Number   99-93351

This publication contains copyrighted material from other sources. Permissions for its use are contained in the "source notes" that precede the "endnotes" at the back of the book. This material may not be further reproduced without the consent of the original owner. Additionally, every effort has been made to reach all the owners of copyrighted material. Any who may have been missed should identify themselves now to negotiate the appropriate permission agreements.

Cover art © 1999 by Edward Molina

Edited by Dr. Mary Beth Poole
Proofread by Martha B. Spencer

Second printing, United States of America, December 1999

This book is dedicated to the enlisted infantrymen of both World Wars and Korea. May the common sense with which they secured victory finally come to be viewed as the foundation of all military knowledge.

Contents

Contents

Maps and Tables

Foreword

John Poole's immensely influential previous book, *The Last Hundred Yards: The NCO's Contribution to Warfare,* filled a gaping hole in Marine Corps literature. It gave Marines, for the first time, a book about modern combat techniques.

This book, *One More Bridge to Cross,* is in effect a prequel to *The Last Hundred Yards.* It places the combat techniques offered in the first book in a larger context. That context is saving lives.

Nothing hits Marines harder than the death of another Marine. The tightly bound nature of the Marine "band of brothers" ensures that every casualty is felt personally by every other Marine. It is not merely for tradition's sake that Marines always recover their dead. Even in death, a Marine is still a Marine, and he is not abandoned to the enemy.

John Poole's work, in this book and in its predecessor, can do a great deal to save Marine lives. The combat techniques and training methods he offers are greatly advanced over those in the official Marine Corps technique manuals. Sadly, the latter often reflect a battlefield devoid of both machineguns and indirect artillery fire. One former Marine officer, now a noted military historian, told me the techniques he learned at The Basic School in the 1980's were straight from the Russo-Japanese War of 1905. I have observed the same myself in Marine Corps field exercises, including on-line attacks similar to the Somme, defenses fully visible to enemy observation and thus doomed to be artillery targets, even on one occasion an attack by a company in column. The only things missing were the shakos [plumed dress hats] and white crossbelts.

But it is not only Marine lives John Poole is concerned about. He wants Marines to wage war in such a way as to spare enemy lives as well, military and civilian.

Some may view this as unmilitary softness. In fact, it reflects a profound understanding of the art of war. Colonel John Boyd, the greatest American military theorist of the 20th century, observed that war is waged at three levels: the physical, the mental and the moral. The physical level — killing people and blowing things up — is the least powerful level. The mental level, where maneuver warfare is largely waged — getting inside the other guy's head — is more powerful than the physical. But the moral level is the most powerful level of all. It is here that guerrilla war is waged, and it is here that sparing enemy lives can pay great dividends. An enemy whose homes are bombed, families killed and soldiers slaughtered gets angry. He wants revenge. The conflict becomes a blood feud, and it cannot be settled until our blood is spilled along with his.

In contrast, a war of maneuver that is relatively bloodless makes peace easier. After the 1940 campaign, the Germans found the French population [to be] largely indifferent and seldom hostile. Part of the reason is that the German *Blitzkrieg* inflicted little physical damage on France. In contrast, the Allied campaign to retake France in 1944, with its typical American emphasis on bombing and mass firepower, inflicted tremendous damage. Not infrequently, German troops had to protect shot-down Allied air-crews from enraged French civilians — a point which German propaganda used to good effect.

In this book, the theme of saving lives has an important subtext: a small unit, a squad or even a fire team, that is properly trained in modern, post-machinegun techniques can be just as effective as a much larger unit, while offering the enemy fewer targets. The German Army, which excelled in drawing lessons from its combat experiences, found as early as World War I that the only difference between a squad attacking a machinegun position and a company doing so was in the number of casualties suffered. Not surprisingly, by 1918 the *Stosstrupp,* a squad-sized unit, was the basic German tactical building block. In contrast, in most Marine infantry units today, the squad is regarded as merely a subset of the platoon, seldom trained for independent action. The result, in combat, is likely to be a lot of dead Marines, Marines whose deaths could have been avoided if tasks were assigned to smaller units.

Those who read *One More Bridge to Cross* merely to discover more combat or training techniques will have missed the point. This is a book about something more, about waging war morally. The God of battles respects those who in turn respect His laws. He also favors those who fight smart. On both counts, John Poole has done the Marine Corps an immense service.

— William S. Lind
(author of *Maneuver Warfare Handbook* and personal advisor to 29th Marine commandant)

Preface

On a foggy September morning in 1944, 35,000 proud young paratroopers departed Britain on the largest airborne invasion ever attempted: Operation "Market-Garden." Three divisions — the U.S. 82nd and 101st, and the British 1st — were to overleap enemy forces retreating across Holland, secure a string of bridges leading into Germany, be reinforced by British XXX Corps armor, and thereby outflank Hitler's Westwall. The 82nd had, as its most difficult objective, the bridge over the Waal River at Nijmegen. Before that bridge was finally taken, elements of the American 504th Infantry Regiment had to move across open ground (and water) into enemy machinegun fire more than once.[1]

Those brave soldiers paid a terrible price for the Nijmegen bridge, but to understand what happened there and in other battles, one must look beyond casualty approximation comparisons. After PVT Billy Yank and SGT Johnny Reb succumbed to their horrific gunshot wounds in Holland, their parents in Elyria, Ohio and Flat Rock, Alabama could do little more than attribute their tragic loss to "the necessary evils of war." But after almost 100 elite U.S. soldiers got killed or wounded by Somali irregulars in a single incident in 1993, American mothers and fathers started to wonder if their offspring had been taught enough about close combat. They didn't totally buy into the military's explanation that too few U.S. tanks had been sent to Mogadishu. They prayed that the U.S. military-industrial complex had remembered to show its infantrymen how to operate without a lot of expensive ordnance. After all, neither the North Koreans nor the North Vietnamese had needed any tanks or planes whatsoever to fight the world's most technologically advanced nation to a standstill. Far from naive, U.S. parents suspected that an overwhelming edge in firepower could pave the way for infantry only in the desert. Could there be one more bridge to cross

— possibly in the realm of small-unit training or tactics — before "the world's smartest" fighting force will be able to occupy enemy territory without extensive loss of life?

Of course, everyone's dream is an end to war altogether. That goal can only be realized incrementally; the chasm between "total war" and "no war" is too wide. First, the common ground between war and morality must be found. Both sides generally have rules to protect prisoners and noncombatants, yet their soldiers still commit atrocities. Partially to blame is man's wounded nature.[2] His flaws must be controlled, but not to the extent that his divine spark is extinguished. What society must guard against is organized inhumanity in the name of expediency. In most religions, there is the belief that God offers man the strength to resist temptation.

Just as individuals struggle to do the right thing, so too do military organizations and government agencies. It is those individuals, organizations, and agencies that view internal discord as disruptive that are the most likely to err. This book is about preserving this country's most valued asset — its youth. A great president once warned of the only real threat to America.

> All the armies of Europe, Asia, and Africa combined . . . could not, by force, take a drink from the Ohio. . . .
> At what point, then, is the approach of danger to be expected? I answer, if it ever reach us, it must spring up amongst us; it cannot come from abroad.[3]
> — Abraham Lincoln
> from "Perpetuation of Our Political Institutions"

If Lincoln were alive today, which would concern him more — evolving standards of behavior and political dissent, or misplaced corporate priorities and inept government bureaucracy? Do not the major political parties base their platforms on monitoring either big business or government? As the battlefield continues to change, must not the U.S. military seek out new ways to cut its losses — in both life and morality? Without realizing that opposing styles of warfare exist, military planners could misinterpret the lessons of history. If America is to continue as the world's peacekeeper, its soldiers and small infantry units must learn how to handle opposition like policemen do — with minimal force.

Acknowledgments

Most of the credit for this work must again go to the United States Marine Corps. From May 1997 through May 1999, commanders of one school, fourteen infantry, three combat-support, and four combat-service-support battalions allowed the author to conduct multiday training sessions on the warfighting methods contained in *The Last Hundred Yards: The NCO's Contribution to Warfare* — a U.S. small-unit tactics manual supplement. Every participant helped to develop the paradoxical training methodology contained herein. Those trips would not have been possible without funding from the Marine Corps University Foundation. Thanks also to Bill Lind and all U.S. service personnel who continue to push for military reform.

Words can't adequately express the author's admiration for those who personally participated in the battles discussed in this book. It is their integrity, courage, and common sense that must be preserved for posterity. Semper fidelis.

Part One

A Heritage Worth Preserving

Only the truth will make you free.
— Pope John Paul II

1 Home of the Free

- *What have been the foremost feats of America?*
- *Which values helped leaders to do the right thing?*

(Source: Courtesy of Edward Molina)

A Tradition of Integrity

On darkened porches throughout the long, hot summer of 1940, Americans sat glued to their radios. Their beloved president had fulfilled his sacred responsibility to them. With regard to foreign policy, he had found the common ground between obeying the law and doing the right thing.

Two major transactions, arranged to skirt the NEUTRALITY ACT of 1935, preceded Lend-Lease. In June 1940, after the evacuation of DUNKIRK, the United States sent "surplus" munitions — worth about $43,000,000 but technically not sold — to England, which was suffering a shortage of ammunition. And in Sept. 1940 the United States authorized the DESTROYERS FOR BASES DEAL that transferred fifty overage destroyers to England in exchange for ninety-nine-year leases to set up air and naval bases in Newfoundland, British Guinea, Bermuda, the Bahamas, Jamaica, St. Lucia, Trinidad, and Antigua.[1]

Because U.S. citizens have always tried to do the right thing, they see integrity as their most enduring quality. What they have accomplished since those uncertain pre-WWII days has defined their national character. Their top priority has become the preservation of life and liberty.

> We hold these truths to be self evident, that all men are created equal, and that they are endowed by their Creator with certain unalienable Rights, that among these are Life, Liberty, and the pursuit of Happiness.[2]
> — *Declaration of Independence*

Preserving Human Life

The intention to save human life has manifested itself in many ways. To help U.S. servicemen and women to survive during WWII, the whole nation mobilized. Those not in uniform bought war bonds, rationed gasoline, raised victory gardens, and took defense industry jobs.

> The women responded. By 1943 they constituted nearly a third of the total work force. Among those who did not take jobs, many managed to make a contribution of another kind through volunteer work. . . .
> More than three million joined the Red Cross to run canteens or serve as nurse's aides or drive ambulances. And more than one million others provided food, entertainment, company and good cheer for lonely servicemen at USO centers across the nation.[3]

By 1943, there were almost three million American boys and girls on the job in American fields and factories, half a million of them in defense plants where they were paid at the standard rate.[4]

(Source: Corel Gallery Clipart, Landmark, 26C028)

To save European refugees after WWII from hunger, chaos, and Communist subversion, American leaders launched the Marshall Plan.

> ... [T]hese men [mostly Wall Street bankers and diplomats] persuaded Congress to help rescue Europe with $13.3 billion in economic assistance over three years. That sum — more than $100 billion in today's dollars, or about six times what America now spends annually on foreign aid — seems unthinkable today. Announced 50 years ago next week, the European Recovery Program, better known as the Marshall Plan, was an extraordinary act of strategic generosity. ... Perhaps America's best export was hope. ... Forced to work together, Europeans overcame some historic enmities while America shed its tradition of peacetime isolationism. Ties strengthened by the Marshall Plan evolved into the Western Alliance. ... It was "one of the greatest and most honorable adventures in history," wrote Dean Acheson [Under-Secretary of State].[5]
> — *Newsweek* (2 June 1997)

Safeguarding Liberty

U.S. leaders have worked equally hard to safeguard liberty around the world. When the Soviets blocked the roads and shut off the electricity to Berlin, they answered with the Berlin Airlift.

> In a steady stream, the cargo planes roared into and out of the city around the clock from June 1948 until August 1949 — one landing every three minutes, one taking off every three minutes. ... These planes carried coal and food and even shipped the parts for an entire power plant to end reliance on the Soviets to keep the lights on. More than one quarter of a million flights were completed and two million tons of cargo were shipped.[6]
> — *Armed Forces Journal* (May 1998)

When the North Koreans invaded the South in 1950, U.S. forces spearheaded the U.N. counteroffensive. After a brilliant strike at Inchon, they advanced all the way to the Chinese border.

> The first ROK forces reached the Yalu on October 25 [1950] and sent back a bottle of its intoxicating waters to Syngman Rhee. Some soldiers, like their American counterparts, equally symbolically chose to urinate from its banks.[7]

Then some 15 years later, while again trying to preserve freedom by shortstopping the "domino effect" of Communism, Americans embarked on their longest war — Vietnam. Large numbers of U.S. ground forces reinforced U.S. military advisors in 1965. For eight years, those forces proved that they could take and hold key terrain. Only after the war's Vietnamization in 1973 did it take a turn for the worse.

> In a series of decisions that extended from April to July [1965], Johnson committed American ground forces to South Vietnam by approving proposals from Westmoreland that would put the equivalent of five American divisions (forty-four maneuver battalions) into the battle.[8]

> After the signing of the Paris Peace Accords, little peace and no accord found their way to South Vietnam, and in March-May 1975 the North Vietnamese army delivered the coup de grace to the Republic of Vietnam. Military pressure and spreading demoralization, in part traceable to a decline in American aid, combined to bring down the Saigon Regime.[9]

Finally, to stamp out evil once and for all, America persevered with the Cold War until its arms race bankrupted the Soviet Union in 1989.

American Intentions Have Always Been Honorable

When a country is fighting for its life against someone as demented as Hitler or Stalin, difficult decisions have to be made. While the impact of those decisions can now be reassessed, their original intent can never be impugned.

If contemporary Americans were asked how to best preserve life and liberty, most would come back with a twofold answer: (1) a continual search for peace, and (2) the minimization of suffering in war. In today's more technologically sophisticated world, total war is no longer a viable option.

Land of the Brave

- *How did the U.S. military develop its proud heritage?*
- *For which ideals have U.S. service personnel fought?*

(Source: FM 22-100 (1983), p. 225)

A Proud Tradition

Most official war records reveal the same distinguished story —
"with more wherewithal, U.S. forces seized their objectives and ex-
acted a heavier toll from their adversary." An abbreviated battle
chronicle from each of America's major wars will illustrate the point.

On 12 December 1861, 113,000 Federal troops crossed the
Rappahannock under fire and subsequently took the town of
Fredericksburg. As they did so, 75,000 Confederates withdrew to
positions behind the town. On the 13th, Franklin's Grand Division
renewed the battle and breached "Stonewall" Jackson's line.[1]

Almost 60 years later on 2 June 1918 at Belleau Wood, U.S. Marines halted the spearhead of the second of the highly successful German Spring offensives. With the French Army in full retreat, they very probably saved Paris. The Marines lost 5199 dead or wounded at Belleau Wood, but not until five German divisions had been declared "unfit for further combat" by their commanders.[2]

As World War II reached its final stages, American units stopped and then decimated in less than a month the best Hitler had to offer at the Battle of the Bulge. Some estimates put German losses at 20,000 higher than American losses.[3]

In Korea during the first few months of 1951, the new U.S. ground commander counterattacked to dispel forever the myth of Chinese invincibility.

Ridgway's army jumped off on the next phase of the advance, Operation Killer, on February 21. By March 1 they had closed up the UN line south of the Han [River], driving back the Chinese with huge casualties. . . .[4]

(Source: FM 7-11B/11C/CM (1979), cover)

During the Vietnam War, on Operation "Maui Peak" in October of 1968, only three U.S. Marine battalions were needed to lift the siege of a U.S. Special Forces Camp by three North Vietnamese Army (NVA) regiments.

> According to a Marine intelligence analysis of 15 September, three North Vietnamese Regiments, the 31st, 21st, and 141st were in position to pose a threat to Thuong Duc.[5]
> — *The Marines in Vietnam 1968*
> Marine Corps History and Museums Division

(Source: FM 100-20 (1981), p. 178)

In the Gulf War at Khafji, an Iraqi armored invasion of Saudi Arabia was deflected without losing a single American life. With the help of airpower, U.S. forces on the ground easily blunted the attack.

Then, American troops were needed in Somalia to restore order and save its people from starvation. To contain the most problematic warlord, those troops finally had to fight. Late in the afternoon of Sunday, 3 October 1993, attack helicopters dropped about 120 of the U.S. Army's best soldiers into a busy neighborhood of Mogadishu to abduct some of Mohammed Farrah Aidid's top lieutenants. When they ran into trouble, an armored column was sent to their assistance. Before the sun rose again over East Africa, Aidid's militia had paid dearly for its indiscretion.

The Red Cross estimated Somali casualties at roughly 1000.[6]
— PBS Program *Frontline*

Ideals for Which They Fought

Those who participated in these battles did so for ideals. In all probability, they were fighting for (1) world welfare, (2) country and Corps, or (3) each other. One can only hope that their sacrifice was actually required to produce the desired result. Contemporary soldiers share these same ideals.

3 With Liberty and Justice for All

- *How has the U.S. gone about freeing the oppressed?*
- *Has it safeguarded its infantrymen in the process?*

(Source: Corel Gallery Clipart, Weapons, 45A038)

The Best Support Available

With the world's largest defense industry, U.S. forces have enjoyed a firepower advantage throughout most of the twentieth century. And they freely expend their limitless supply of ordnance to preserve the lives of their soldiers. To win, they aim their biggest weapons at the largest concentrations of enemy. Because hilltops afford air and artillery observers the best view, they are often the ground attack objectives. Every effort is made to safely overwhelm any that are occupied. All operations are carefully controlled from the top. At the bottom, accidental shootings are virtually eliminated by strict adherence to alignment — no single soldier or element advancing faster than any other. In fact, U.S. forces have become very proficient at methodically destroying whatever gets in their way. By attacking across a wide frontage in the daytime, commanders maintain absolute control over their units. Those units seldom hide and never retreat. They fight in the open with honor and have little respect for those who resort to guerrilla tactics.

> There is another type of warfare — new in its intensity, ancient in its origin — war by guerrillas, subversives, insurgents, assassins; war by ambush instead of by combat, by infiltration instead of aggression, seeking victory by eroding and exhausting the enemy instead of engaging him.[1]
> — President John F. Kennedy

To draw a line in the sand and then dare any opponent to cross it has become the American tradition. U.S. commanders do so to increase their chances of killing large numbers of enemy. They are willing to dedicate as much time and ordnance as necessary to winning. This way of fighting is called "attrition warfare."

(Source: FM 5-103 (1985), p. 4-3)

Technology's Promise

To save more lives, Americans have become proficient at fighting wars from long range. To cripple enemy supply lines and pave the way for infantry, they have come to depend heavily on aerial and artillery bombardment. Any weapon with standoff capability — from tanks that detect enemy heat signatures to rifles that project infrared-dot targets — has a market. U.S. citizens have come to believe that "smart" bombs and missiles can return some semblance of morality to the battlefield.

(Source: FM 7-85 (1987), p. 7-12)

Still Questions Linger

A few questions have yet to be answered satisfactorily. For example, how can safeguarding the inhabitants of an occupied nation be balanced against properly preparing a troop-landing site with supporting-arms fire? Or on a smaller scale, how can enemy hostages be saved without putting them at risk? And, then there is the age-old question — can enemy territory be occupied without losing large numbers of infantrymen?

Part Two

How Wars Are Won

To correctly assess what has occurred on the field of honor, we must discover the truth — the whole, hard, irrevocable truth. Until we as a nation acknowledge the truth, we dishonor all who have given their lives for our freedom and jeopardize those who still serve.
— an anonymous U.S. war veteran

4 One Nation under God

- *Did moral theology help to shape national identity?*
- *Have these religious values always been followed?*

(Source: Cover of ☐Christian Truth and Its Defense,☐ copyright ' 1997 by David E. Bishop)

Christian Values Have Shaped America

Of the six billion people who inhabit this planet, roughly nine tenths believe in God. Even Hinduism is monotheistic — with Brahma, Vishnu, and Shiva forming a type of trinity,[1] and the multitude of lesser deities looking a lot like angels. God has been talking to all of his children since the beginning of time. One can find His message — "it is in giving that you will receive" — on ancient inscriptions throughout the world.

Hatred is never appeased by hatred in this world.

By non-hatred alone is hatred appeased. This is a law eter-
nal.[2]
> — inscription from stupa ruins at Sarnath, India
> where the "enlightened" Buddha first preached

Thus, while not all Americans are Christians per se, most es-
pouse Christian ideals; and most can relate to moral theology as
discussed from a Christian standpoint. Most who believe in a Su-
preme Being personifying good also believe in a counterspirit personifying evil. Because the "evil one" has been universally described
as the "great deceiver," it should come as no surprise that much of
what appears to be true in the world really isn't. Only by examining a topic from the standpoint of moral theology can one begin to
understand all there is to know about that topic.

Inversely, where partial truth exists, one should not be surprised
to find collateral shortfalls in morality. God is truth. Where truth
is absent, so is God.

I am the way, the truth, and the life.[3]
> — Jesus (as quoted by His apostle John)

God has truly blessed this nation. U.S. citizens have one of the
highest standards of living in the world and something that few
others enjoy — hope. Whatever their social or economic status at
birth, they can work to achieve something better. If these blessings
had been restricted to peacetime, Navy chaplains would not have
as their motto that "faith is courage." Many veterans believe that
the winning of WWII was a miracle. While they fought to preserve
democracy and free enterprise, most openly admit that both have
their pitfalls. They didn't shed their precious blood so fellow Americans could do as they like; they fought so future generations could
enjoy responsible freedom. Was it not unfettered freedom — in the
form of hedonism — that led to the demise of the Roman Empire?

If responsible freedom is the goal, human life takes precedence
over economic gain. If traditional values are eroding, Americans
must ask themselves why. For theological insight, there is no better source than organized religion.

So called *moral permissiveness* rests on an erroneous conception of human freedom; the necessary precondition for the development of true freedom is to let oneself be educated in the moral law. Those in charge of education can reasonably be expected to give young people instruction respectful of truth, the qualities of heart, and the moral and spiritual dignity of man.[4]

How Much Freedom Was Intended

The free-enterprise system holds great promise, but also inherent risk. If, by chance, money actually is "the root of all evil," how it is made and used has to be monitored by society. Tobacco smoke causes cancer, yet the cigarette makers still fight its regulation. "Gasohol" produces fewer carcinogens than gasoline. Why isn't its manufacture and distribution subsidized? Alcohol can be made relatively cheaply from any surplus agricultural commodity; the only real cost lies in transporting it from the mid-West. Petroleum-poor Brazilians have been running their cars on sugarcane alcohol for 70 years. In short, big business has been slow to tell Americans the whole story, and big government has been slow to call them on it.

> . . . [T]hat Spirit of Truth whom the world can never receive since it neither sees nor knows Him.[5]
> — John 14:17

One of the biggest moneymakers in America has been arms manufacturing. By some estimates, gun stores outnumber gas stations on U.S. streets. It's doubtful that the drafters of the Second Amendment to the Constitution thought it necessary for every man, woman, and child to have his or her own gun.

> [About] 230,000,000 guns are in circulation in the U.S. today, says the ATF.[6]
> — *Newsweek* (31 May 1999)

In November 1998, the mayor of crime-ridden New Orleans attempted to recover the costs of gun-related violence from firearms manufacturers. Then, the mayors of Chicago and Miami did likewise. When the mayor of Atlanta tried it, the state legislature banned all such lawsuits.[7] Those brave mayors may have set a precedent with far-reaching implications.

> The U.S. leads the world in the value of arms exported to other governments. . . . Among industrialized nations, the U.S. has the second highest murder rate . . . and the most handgun deaths. . . . We are still the biggest consumers of . . . gasoline. . . . We also have the world's largest petroleum refinery capacity. In terms of per capita energy consumption, we are second only to the United Arab Emirates.[8]
> — *Parade Magazine* (13 April 1997)

What the average American is just now starting to realize is that an excess of oversized guns can create problems too. Being the biggest seller of military arms to other nations does little to champion human rights or promote world peace.

> Amnesty International USA today released its 1997 report on the state of human rights around the world, with a presentation by its executive director William F. Shulz. . . .
> . . . In his testimony before the congressional human rights caucus, the Rev. Dr. Shulz really went to town on the sins of the U.S. administration. "The United States hypocrisy is evident," he declared. "It represents itself as a champion of freedom, democracy and human rights while providing arms to countries like Colombia, Turkey and Israel."[9]
> — *Hindustan Times* (19 June 1997)

> *The production and the sale of arms* affect the common good of nations and of the international community. Hence public authorities have the right and duty to regulate them. The short-term pursuit of private or collective interests cannot legitimate undertakings that promote violence and conflict among nations and compromise the international juridical order.[10]

The *accumulation of arms* strikes many as a paradoxically suitable way of deterring potential adversaries from war.

They see it as the most effective means of ensuring peace among nations. This method of deterrence gives rise to strong moral reservations. The *arms race* does not ensure peace. Far from eliminating the causes of war, it risks aggravating them. Spending enormous sums to produce ever new type of weapons impedes efforts to aid needy populations (Cf. Paul VI, *PP 53);* it thwarts the development of peoples. *Over-armament* multiplies reasons for conflict and increases the danger of escalation.[11]

While the U.S. has on occasion used its military arsenal to help the rest of the world, it is still only one country in a community of nations. Its success in leading those nations toward a more prosperous and peaceful future will largely depend on how they perceive America. Being the biggest and richest kid on the block makes it harder to create a good impression. On the world stage, opponents often portray themselves as peace-loving nations being bullied by the world's greatest military power. Retaliatory excesses do little to dispel that claim.

(Source: Corel Gallery Clipart, weapons 45A097)

Are Americans at a Fork in the Trail?

The Bible warns that morality and legality don't always coincide. In pre-Civil War America, it was legal to kill suspicious Indians and runaway slaves. In WWII Germany, it was legal to exterminate Jews. One wonders how much of what contemporary Americans can get away with, actually violates morality.

A Closer Look
at History

● *Is there more to the story?*

● *Have U.S. units really done as well as purported?*

(Source: FM 22-100 (1983), p. 12)

The Rest of the Story

Only certain aspects of U.S. military training have been categorically "the best" in the world. It's true that U.S. infantrymen have become adept at employing their weapons and following orders. Their pride and courage are so carefully nurtured that many come to believe that bullets won't hurt them.

While this country expends unlimited ordnance on behalf of its infantrymen, this ordnance does them less good than is generally acknowledged. Because of what a single machinegunner can do, bombardment can no longer pave the way for infantry. After 576 tons of oversized bombs were dropped from 147 B-17 and 82 B-25 bombers on the Monte Casino abbey in Italy during WWII, subsequent infantry assaults still failed.[1]

For most individual ground actions, published casualty ratios usually favor the U.S., but enemy losses are often the product of hastily counted bodies and subsequent bombing approximations. How many soldiers get killed has little to do with a war's outcome anyway. Victory depends more on what happens to strategic targets. Heavy American losses always seem to be reported in the context of heavier enemy losses. Yet, questions remain. How can opposition fatalities be accurately assessed when U.S. infantrymen rarely see who they are fighting? Since WWII, veterans have repeatedly made this claim — among them one from vegetated Vietnam,[2] and the following two from barren Iwo Jima:

> We hardly ever saw an enemy [on Iwo Jima]. The Japanese had every inch of ground covered by fire.[3]
> — Navaho Marine veteran
> "Japanese Codetalkers" on History Channel

> Seldom on Iwo, from D-day until the battle was over [36 days later], did you see the enemy — just the sights and sounds of deadly fire from his weapons. You could see comrades moving and hear the shouted commands of officers and noncoms. And, once the attack began, you soon would hear those terrible cries of "Corpsman! Corpsman!"[4]
> — Marine infantryman on Iwo Jima

Even if enemy casualty counts had been roughly accurate, one wonders what portion might have been "civilian sympathizers" or forced laborers. It is, after all, well known that the Japanese used Korean laborers throughout the Pacific.

The Foe Didn't Always Pay More Heavily

A closer look at the seven battles in Chapter 2 reveals a slightly different story. Additional details can sometimes put solitary facts into better perspective.

Fredericksburg

Stonewall Jackson's line was only temporarily breached behind Fredericksburg. Then, when Gen. Burnside renewed his attack, he established something of a precedent. With fourteen unsuccessful frontal assaults on Marye's Heights,[5] he managed to sacrifice the cream of the Union army (including the Irish Brigade).

In the one-sided killing match the North had 12,600 casualties, the South fewer than 5000.[6]

Belleau Wood

In a tragic replay of what had happened at Gettysburg, U.S. Marines had to cross 800 yards of open wheatfield just to enter Belleau Wood during WWI. This does little to bolster one's conviction that 5199 U.S. casualties were necessary to stop the German offensive.

> Gen. Krulak said he took his first walk a year ago, starting near the town of Lucy-le-Bocage, where the WWI marines launched their attack June 6.
> "I walked toward the tree line through waist-high wheat, just as they did 80 years ago," the Commandant said. "History books describe that 800-yard advance, but I never fully appreciated it until I walked it myself. The Germans had every square inch of that field covered by machinegun and artillery fire. The Marines paid dearly with every step they took."[7]
> — *Leatherneck Magazine* (August 1998)

> This [Thursday, 6 June] would be the most catastrophic day in Marine Corps history. More Marines would be killed and wounded on this single day than in all its previous existence. . . . For all intents and purposes, the old warriors of the U.S. Marine Corps were virtually wiped out, mainly leaving replacements to carry the war to its final term. . . .

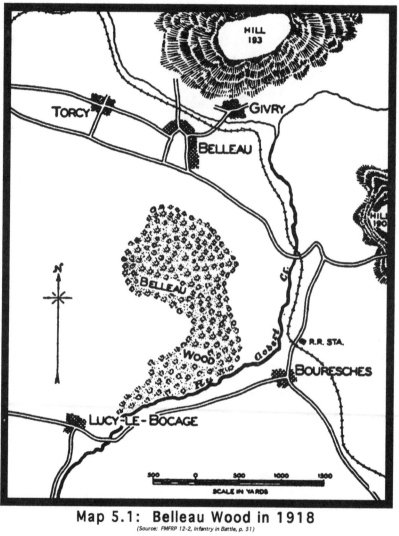

Map 5.1: Belleau Wood in 1918
(Source: FMFRP 12-2, Infantry in Battle, p. 31)

At 1700 five-hundred Marines of the 3d Battalion, Fifth Marines, jumped off . . . with an almost perfect skirmish line. . . .

What was not known officially, mainly because no American reconnaissance had been undertaken beforehand, was that the woods were chock full *[sic]* of Germans and the approaches were thoroughly covered by their artillery. In addition, and more devastating to the Marines, were the many heavy Maxim [machine] guns that had been placed in advantageous, and interlocking positions within the wood. . . .

As soon as 3/5 left its wooded place of safety to cross the open wheatfields lying before them, deadly machine gun fire was encountered. . . . While crossing the open ground to their immediate front the losses to Berry's battalion were terrific. . . .

In just a few short minutes the Third Battalion, Fifth Marines, was just a memory. . . .

According to its semi-official history, 3/6 [3d Battalion, 6th Marines] jumped-off at exactly 1700 from their positions . . . just to the east of Lucy-le-Bocage. . . . In fact, in very short order they ran into a wall of Maxims that 3/5 had [also run into]. . . .

Both the 84th and 97th [companies of 3/6] advanced through open wheatfields [south of Belleau Wood] under constant observation and direct artillery and machine gun fire. . . .

Holcomb's battalion [2/6] received orders at 1630 to jump-off at 1730 with one company. . . .

At 1730 the 96th went forward as ordered. . . . Going through the wheatfield [south of Belleau Wood toward the town of Bouresches], against emplaced, heavy machine guns, and the dreaded shell fire, the losses of the 96th were horrendous. . . .

The 6th of June 1918, was . . . "The longest Day," . . . for the 4th Marine Brigade. The losses for the day, thirty-one officers and 1,056 enlisted men. . . . The largest proportion were suffered in the afternoon among the three battalions engaged, 3/5, 3/6, and 2/6.[8]

The Battle of the Bulge

As for what happened in WWII, U.S. forces paid a higher price in the Battle of the Bulge than most Americans realize. The fight for the Hurtgen Forest in November set the tone for what was to come.

> By mid November, the 28th [Division] was so badly chewed up that it was relieved and sent to the quiet Ardennes front for rest and rehabilitation. It was replaced in Hurtgen Forest by the 8th Division; then the 8th too was badly mauled. . . .
> . . . A regiment of the 1st Division took a pounding in the northern fringe of the forest. The 4th Division suffered such heavy losses that, like the 28th, it was pulled out and sent to the quiet Ardennes front for repairs. Then the 83rd Division was sent into the deadly forest, followed in turn by the 5th Armored. . . . It was as if the battle had become an end in itself and the American commanders had been hypnotized into making endless sacrifices. . . .
> All told 120,000 men and additional thousands of replacements were fed into the Hurtgen meat grinder. Finally, on 13 December [when the battle ended] . . . more than 24,000 American soldiers had been reported killed, wounded, captured, or missing in action, and another 9,000 had fallen victim to disease or battle fatigue. More than 25 per cent of the Americans who fought in Hurtgen Forest were casualties.[9]

When Hitler then attacked through the Ardennes in mid-December in what came to be known as the "Battle of the Bulge," he had to use hastily assembled and poorly supported *Volksgrenadier* (people's infantry) divisions. How Allied Headquarters reacted to this threat showed little confidence in U.S. infantry capabilities. As with the Hurtgen Forest campaign, they simply pumped large numbers of warm bodies into the path of the Germans — 600,000 to be exact.[10]

Near the end of December, Eisenhower suggested raising Belgian, Polish, and more French divisions, and plans were soon under way for equipping eight French divisions and close to 500,000 men — mostly Frenchmen — to guard the lines of communication. In Washington, at Eisenhower's request, the Joint Chiefs of Staff stepped up the sailing dates of an airborne, three infantry, and three armored divisions to Europe. They also allocated to Eisenhower three more infantry divisions not previously scheduled for his command. General Marshall began to comb out support units in the United States, Alaska, and Panama to provide infantry replacements.

What about transferring divisions from Italy, asked Eisenhower. Perhaps 100,000 U.S. Marines. He set his staff to work on a plan for obtaining volunteers from segregated Negro support units to join the infantry.[11]

Luckily, the 82nd and 101st airborne divisions were nearby recuperating from Operation Market-Garden, and General Patton's 3rd Army was able to turn north on a moment's notice.

When the battle officially ended on 28 January 1945, one source had German casualties at 120,000 and American at 100,000,[12] another had German losses at 100,000 and American at 80,987.[13] More precise and better substantiated estimates tell a different story.

On 8 January 1945, Hitler authorized the retreat of his troops from the tip of the Bulge.[14] From the time the enemy attacked out of the Ardennes until the 1st and 3rd U.S. Armies closed their pincers on a mostly empty salient at Houffalize on 16 January,[15] the Germans suffered 44,420 casualties and the Americans 50,805.[16] If rear security for the retreating German column was only 13 miles from Hitler's Westwall at that time, how many aircraft-inflicted losses the column took for 12 more days is mostly speculation. Casualty statistics are difficult to ascertain from aerial photographs. One author hypothesizes that newly inducted and quickly trained German soldiers did well at the Bulge because of better German leadership. Better small-unit infantry tactics probably had more to do with it.

At the height of the battle for Bastogne, on 4 January 1945, General Patton wrote in his diary: "We can still lose this war. . . . The Germans are colder and hungrier than we are, but they fight better." . . .

I tried to interest the Pentagon in my quantitative finding about German combat performance. I thought that the U.S. Army might learn something useful if it were to study the German Army to find out why it possessed this persistent combat effectiveness superiority. The typical answer I got from Pentagon officials was, "Why study the German Army? We won the war didn't we?" Yes, of course we won the war. We won it because the Allies overwhelmed the Germans with numbers of men and machines. But I still asked why the Germans were better fighters than we were unit for unit. The Pentagon didn't care.[17]

[T]he majority of American divisions needed overwhelming artillery . . . and close air support to best their German opponents.[18]

Operations Killer and Ripper in Korea

When in Korea, the U.S. 8th Army counterattacked during February of 1951, it did so by leveling everything in its path. Because the American infantry units did not match up well in tactical ability with their Communist counterparts, they had little choice but to let supporting arms do their work for them. History records what happened as another meat grinder.[19]

The advance of the seven American divisions now in the line was the twentieth century successor to the Roman "tortoise": instead of long columns, exposed to surprise attack, Ridgway's units now deployed at every stage for all-around defense in depth, securing themselves against infiltration while they waited for the massed artillery and air strikes to do their work upon the Chinese positions. On March 7 Killer was succeeded by Ripper. . . . The envelopment of Seoul by the success of Ripper made the Communist evacuation of the capital inevitable. On March 14 the victors recovered a devastated city, a metropolis of ruins and corrugated iron in which, of the principal buildings, only the Capitol and the railway station survived.[20]

40 million gallons of napalm were used in Korea.[21]
— PBS Special *Korea — the Unknown War*

To the civilians being liberated, Ridgway's tactic must have left something to be desired. They were used to invasion, but this was nothing like anything they had ever seen before.

The North Koreans were like ghosts. They passed over the countryside and left no mark on it in many ways. But when you use the rock crusher techniques of an American army you hurt your friends. And that was true in Vietnam as well as in Korea.[22]
— Maj.Gen. Edwin Simmons USMC (Ret.)
former Director of USMC History and Museums
PBS Special *Korea — the Unknown War*

While South Korean civilians had little experience with intense bombing and shelling, they did with the overuse of small arms. A few had been summarily shot after being suspected of Communist sympathies on Cheju Island in 1948.

The [prewar] South was in trouble. The economy was hurt by high inflation and discontent was widespread. Order was maintained by the police.[23]
— PBS Special *Korea — the Unknown War*

The [South Korean] police were very cruel. They defended where they would. They arrested frequently without warrant. The kind of justice that was dispensed relied very little on rules of evidence. It was not very just, and people were tortured to provide statements for the prosecutors.[24]
— Gregory Henderson
U.S. Vice Counsel to Korea 1948—1950
PBS Special *Korea — the Unknown War*

On the island of Cheju, guerrilla activity was intense. In May 1948, the U.S. military governor General William Dean flew in to supervise [the] counterinsurgency operations. The guerrillas were mainly poor peasants who had taken to arms. Their weapons were often crude but could be lethal. A cycle of revolutionary violence and reprisal was under way. Some 30,000 people were killed on Cheju. In October 1948, a constabulary unit at Yoshu refused to go there and mutinied.[25]
   — PBS Special *Korea — the Unknown War*

Though Kim Je-Hue — the Yoshu rebels battalion commander — had been my student while I was principal of the military academy, I volunteered to command the expedition to suppress the guerrillas in the South Chiri Mountains. It hurt and broke my heart when I shot him and the whole battalion, but they were enemies that wanted our country to become communist and were therefore unforgivable, so I annihilated them before returning to Seoul.[26]
   — Chung Il-Wan
    South Korean Constabulary
    PBS Special *Korea — the Unknown War*

After the North Koreans attacked, Syngman Rhee's soldiers continued to view anyone who had allowed him- or herself to be overrun as a Communist sympathizer.

I took lots of pictures. Inchon was just a sea of rubble. . . . Now don't forget that all of these civilians are being liberated by the South Koreans. I think the South Korean soldiers were mad because they shot at everything that moved. And all these kids and old ladies are walking along with their hands up because they are terrified of these South Korean soldiers.[27]
   — Bert Hardy
    Picture Post Photographer
    PBS Special *Korea — the Unknown War*

The Chinese and North Koreans had little trouble infiltrating through and operating behind Allied lines. Because both had discovered how to harness the common sense of the individual soldier through decentralized control, their tactics closely resembled those of a guerrilla. With the distinction between guerrilla and civilian blurred, Allied forces became tempted to disregard the welfare of the indigenous population. From the shelling of occupied buildings, the problem may have metastasized into the shooting of noncombatants. South Korean civilians in the path of Operations Killer and Ripper had trouble identifying friend from foe.

> The thing that shook me more than anything was to see people — in extreme danger certainly — just shooting indiscriminately and even shooting civilians.[28]
> — Rt.Hon. George Younger M.P.
> Future British Defense Minister
> Then Argyll & Southern Highlander
> PBS Special *Korea — the Unknown War*

Operation Maui Peak in Vietnam

Three NVA regiments may have been in a position to threaten the Thuong Duc Special Forces Camp in October 1968, but in its immediate vicinity were only elements of two. The three Marine battalions that lifted its siege had the help of two Army of the Republic of Vietnam (ARVN) battalions, B-52 strikes, and a foe that disengaged early.[29] They also had the help of a fourth Marine battalion functioning as a decoy several miles to the east. To fully appreciate what happened on Maui Peak, one must know a little of the geography and history of its operational area.

Thuong Duc lay 10 miles west of where Route 4 and the Son Vu Gia River entered the coastal plain. The Corps had prior experience with this valley at the south end of "Charlie Ridge," but most of it had been unpleasant. Because its mouth lay at the western end of the 7th Marines' area of responsibility, leatherneck units had occasionally tried to enter it. Each time, before advancing more than a few hundred yards, they had run into superior numbers of highly skilled and well supported enemy. The side draws and foothills at the base of Charlie Ridge tended to be the most dangerous.

Of the three Marine battalions needed to lift the "siege" of

Thuong Duc, the one that probably saw the most action was used as a diversion at the mouth of this valley — 2d Battalion, 5th Marines. The young Marines of 2/5 fought bravely but had nowhere near the individual or small-unit skills of their opponents. Only hours after taking a heavily contested, pyramid-shaped hill at the foot of Charlie Ridge, Golf company got painfully introduced to enemy counterattack capabilities. In full moonlight on the sparsely vegetated hillside, NVA scouts dressed like bushes managed to get within grenade range by moving slower than is perceptible to the human eye.[30] This fairly warm Maui Peak sideshow eventually ended after it was deemed too dangerous to insert, at the top of the ridge above 2/5's hard-won beachhead, the operation's reserve force — two additional ARVN battalions and a brigade of the U.S. 101st Airborne Division.[31]

Vietnam was America's longest war. Many U.S. citizens to this day believe that more military leeway or Congressional support could have produced a different result. The truth is that the war was lost on the ground. It would have turned out the same way if Hanoi had been occupied. The enemy was using a style of warfare that didn't require airplanes, tanks, or resupply. The only way to win the war was to copy enemy tactics. If the free-fire zones around major U.S. installations had been subdivided into small, well delineated, fireteam-controlled Tactical Areas of Operation (TAOR's), no main force NVA unit could have gotten within rocket range of those installations. Equipped with silenced rifles, four-man groups of U.S. infantry could have been secretly inserted and resupplied. Thoroughly trained in the use of spider holes, supporting arms, claymores, grenades, and microterrain escape routes, these young Americans could have bloodied any number of enemy without disclosing their own presence. If any team had gotten into trouble, a rifle company could have quickly helicoptered in to save them.

Khafji's Defense in the Gulf War

It was a wise decision not to defend Khafji with more than a few well hidden Marine snipers. Long-range fires can accomplish wonders in unobstructed dessert terrain. But why the Iraqi armored column made it all the way to the town — so Saudi soldiers had to evict them — deserves further review. Had those Marine snipers been authorized to run their own air strikes, the town might never have been occupied. One of them — Cpl. Matthew Schott — asserted later that with the authority to request and control his own close air support, he could have single-handedly stopped the tanks.[32] He and his partner did manage to put "metal on metal" with artillery shells. And the city limits do constitute an obvious control feature. The pilots needed only to be told that everything north of the built-up area was fair game.

The Raid into Mogadishu

The U.S. Rangers and Delta Force personnel who raided the Somali warlord's headquarters on the afternoon of 3 Oct 1993 did not get ambushed in the normal sense of the word. They merely got into trouble following the time-honored and outdated U.S. tradition of hastily attacking a prepared enemy position. When those brave soldiers came under counterattack, what they needed were the tactical techniques to defend a piece of urban terrain against superior numbers. They may not have expected the creeping encirclement that Orientals and Africans have used for centuries. Not always able to see who was killing them, they may have resorted to shooting at anything that moved. Their courage and conduct are beyond reproach; what is at issue here is a system that would send its young men into harm's way without first teaching them the lessons of history.

> Late in the afternoon of Sunday, Oct. 3, 1993, attack helicopters dropped about 120 elite American soldiers into a busy neighborhood in the heart of Mogadishu, Somalia. Their mission was to abduct several top lieutenants of Somali warlord Mohammed Farrah Aidid and return to base. It was supposed to take about an hour. . . .
>
> Instead, two of their high-tech UH-60 Blackhawk attack helicopters were shot down. The men were pinned down through a long and terrible night in a hostile city, fighting for their lives. When they emerged the following morning, 18 Americans were dead and 73 wounded. . . .

Carefully defined rules of engagement, calling for soldiers to fire only on Somalis who aimed weapons at them, were quickly discarded in the heat of the fight. Most soldiers interviewed said that through most of the fight they fired on crowds and eventually at anyone and anything they saw. . . .

Official U.S. estimates of Somalian casualties at the time numbered 350 dead and 500 injured [many of which were women and children]. . . . The Task Force Ranger commander, Maj.Gen. William F. Garrison, testifying before the Senate, said that if his men had put any more ammunition into the city "we would have sunk it."[33]

— *Philadelphia [Inquirer] On Line* (November 1997)

Were Ideals Followed?

- To what extent did enemy civilians get in the way?
- Did the U.S. fulfill its obligations to servicemen?

(Source: FMFM 2-1 (1967), p. 115)

Protecting the World's Welfare Has Not Been Pretty

Those who fought for world welfare will be shocked to learn of the slaughter to which their superiors resorted with all good intentions. During WWII, corners were cut trying to damage enemy morale and industrial production. Some 100,000 noncombatants were suffocated or were burned to death in Dresden alone. Four days of British and American fire bombing would be hard to justify even if Dresden had possessed strategic targets — which it didn't. It was a university town containing thousands of refugees from the east.[1] Nothing can prepare the reader for what happened in the Pacific.

Dropping 2000 tons of napalm on Tokyo on the night of
9 March 1945 leveled 16 square miles and killed 100,000
people. . . . The fire bombing of all Japanese cities killed
half a million people.[2]

Takeoffs began at Guam at 5:35 P.M. and 40 minutes
later at Saipan and Tinian. . . . By a quarter past eight, 334
B-29's were in the air . . . heading north.
. . . Pathfinder planes — each carrying a load of 180
napalm-filled, 70-pound canisters — flew over Tokyo on
crossing courses. . . .
Guiding on the X, the main body of B-29's flew over in
groups of three. . . . They carried loads of incendiaries that
automatically fell from the bomb bays a regular intervals.
. . . The target area, about three by five miles in size, included a considerable portion of Tokyo's industrial and commercial districts and a densely packed residential area that
held an average of 103,000 people per square mile.
Hit with string after string of incendiaries, central Tokyo became a holocaust. In the heart of the fire storm, tem-
peratures rose to 1,800° F. Water boiled in the canals criss-
crossing the city. The fire fed upon itself, creating thermal
updrafts that tossed the bombers like errant leaves.
For nearly three hours the B-29's kept coming. Soot
blackened the silver fuselages of the late arrivals, which
were forced to bomb around the fringes of the target area to
avoid the turbulence and the blinding smoke that filled cock-
pits with the stench of burning wood, flesh and hair.
One pilot, keeping a hand on the wheel, crossed himself
with the other and was heard to say, "This blaze will haunt
me forever. It's the most terrifying sight in the world. . . ."
The official Japanese count, which took 25 days to complete, was 83,793 killed and 40,918 injured. . . . From reconnaissance photos, LeMay could count 15.8 square miles re-
duced to ashes, including 18 percent of the industrial area,
and 63 percent of the commercial center.[3]
— "Bombers over Japan"
Time-Life Books

Contemporary Americans shouldn't stand in judgment of those forced to counter superior infantry tactics with overwhelming firepower in the past, but they should demand a different response in the future. Those who insist on the moral correctness of heavily bombing population centers should consider the history of the second atomic target. Nagasaki had been the center of European and Christian influence in Japan and home to many of the 200,000 to 300,000 Christians martyred after Japan closed its doors to the Western World in 1650.[4] When Japan reopened those doors in 1858, 20,000 residents of Kyushu (Nagasaki's home island) were found to be secretly practicing Christianity.[5] But the bomb still happened.

U.S. air power had trouble interdicting enemy supply lines in Korea, because the Communists could carry in most of what they needed on their backs. This shouldn't have surprised U.S. planners. Toward the end of WWII, the builders of the Burma Road had quantified how much less a Chinese division needed to operate.

> China had learned to fight economically. An American division needs roughly 5,000 tons of supplies to enable it to fight for thirty days; an equivalent Chinese division can get along on 600 tons.[6]

In Korea, much of the Communist resupply effort consisted of thousands of coolies moving back and forth along a myriad of trails. As such, it was relatively immune to bombing. This removed from the aerial bombardment most of its justification.

> The terrible irony of the bombing of N. Korea was that it didn't affect the war effort. . . . We never found a way to stop their supply lines for example. These little guys with A-frames on their backs carrying several hundred pounds of supplies could not be hit by bombing. The reason for this is very simple. It goes back to the bombing survey done of WWII . . . [in which it was found] that German industrial production went up rather than down in the context of the bombing. Bombing is not an effective strategy for ending a war or stopping supply lines.[7]
> — Professor Bruce Cumings
> PBS Special *Korea — the Unknown War*

600,000 tons of bombs fell on N. Korea. Possibly 2 million
civilians perished.[8]
— PBS Special *Korea — the Unknown War*

Not known for dwelling on past mistakes, America's war planners then proceeded to repeat this one — for the third time in 25
years — in Vietnam. The error had become so predictable that
Chesty Puller saw it coming.

When I later asked whether we could do so [defeat the North
Vietnamese] by bombing, he [Chesty Puller] suggested I read
the *Strategic Bombing Survey* done immediately after World
War II, keeping in mind that North Vietnam was an agrar-
ian nation.[9]
— Son-in-law of Lt.Gen. Lewis B. Puller USMC(Ret.)
from 1957 interview with the Marine legend

With skilled infantrymen, the North Vietnamese didn't need as much
wherewithal to pursue their war aims. Whatever materiel they
couldn't take from their oversupplied opponent, they brought down
countless jungle trails by bicycle. As in Korea, their "supply lines"
were virtually immune to interdiction from the sky.

A five-hundred-mile jungle supply route led from the North
through Laos and Cambodia. Down it came a stream of
trucks carrying food and weapons. . . . Because the risk of
air attacks increased as they went south, supplies had to be
unloaded and moved along by other means. "Each of the
four bags of rice I carried weighed 100 kilos. I put two bags
at each end of a pole and tied them together with a piece of
string. As I walked uphill, I pushed the bike along with
another pole against my shoulder," [said a female porter].[10]
— "Guerrilla Wars"
PBS Special *Peoples' Century*

. . . [R]ound-the-clock B-52 bombing missions and jet fighter
interdiction and strafing operations were obviously not working. Although a B-52 could unleash over 100 750-lb. bombs

within 30 seconds, cutting a huge swathe through the target area, the estimated cost to the infiltrators of this devastating firepower was only one death to every 300 bombs.[11]

On an average day, U.S. artillery expended 10,000 or so rounds. . . . The total tonnage of bombs dropped over North Vietnam, South Vietnam, Cambodia, and Laos came to about 8 million (about four times the tonnage used in all of World War II).[12]
— *Vietnam War Almanac*

This process of systematic destruction was not just used on the Ho Chi Minh Trail complex in remote sections of eastern Laos and Cambodia; it was also applied to populated areas of the country being "liberated."

To deprive the Viet Cong of anywhere to hide, whole areas were cleared. Mao had told the guerrillas to move like fish in water, so the American forces tried to drain that water. Once the villagers had left, soldiers made sure there was nothing to come back to. And they tried to remove the guerrillas' cover in the forests. Hundreds of thousands of tons of napalm, high-explosive phosphorous bombs, and agent orange defoliant were dropped. And when all other tactics seemed to be failing, the bombing was stepped up. The South Vietnamese people found it hard to believe the government's line that the destruction was necessary to save their country. Over a million civilians lost their lives.[13]
— "Guerrilla Wars"
PBS Special *Peoples' Century*

After watching the U.S. military make the same mistake over and over, one wonders how powerful the U.S. arms-manufacturing lobby has really become. Today's "smart" bombs better hit what they are aimed at, but have yet to solve the problems of target dispersal or identification. For foolproof target acquisition, one needs small teams of infantrymen with enough skill to covertly approach a target along the ground.

Country and Corps Have Been Fickle Mistresses

Many who fought for country and Corps have since become somewhat disillusioned. National policy mistakes have been exposed and enemy capabilities declassified. Many veterans suspect that they weren't told everything they needed to know to survive their life-and-death struggle. When the voting public realizes that it has also been protected from the whole story, some long-overdue changes may be possible. Anxious to avoid being accused of lack of foresight or negligence, authorities will sometimes prolong a state of ignorance, and organizations will sometimes censor information. Gandhi warned that "too many secrets erode democracy,"[14] Pope John Paul II that "only the truth will make you free."[15]

Most infantry veterans have had unpleasant experiences with U.S. firepower. Some of those millions of bombs and shells end up hitting the wrong people. Detailed statistics on how many U.S. servicemen have been injured this way are not readily available. As the origin of each incoming round is often difficult to determine, any number of casualties from "friendly fire" may have been attributed to combat action.

> As our [U.S. Army] study shook out, the fact became inescapable that a staggering 15 to 20 percent of all U.S. casualties in Vietnam were caused by friendly fire.[16]
> — Col. David H. Hackworth U.S. Army (Ret.)
> most highly decorated Vietnam War veteran

(Source: Corel Gallery Clipart, People 34H008)

The Defense Department's official casualty report for the Vietnam War lists 45,958 combat deaths and 10,303 nonhostile deaths for the period between January 1, 1961 and March 31, 1973.[17]

About 18 percent of U.S. fatalities were from causes other than enemy action. . . .[18]

— *Encyclopedia of the Vietnam War*

Some 51 percent of U.S. Army combat deaths [in Vietnam] were caused by [enemy] small-arms fire, more than from any other cause; 35 percent were caused by fragments from [enemy] artillery and mortar shells, rockets, and grenades. In contrast, during World War II and the Korean War only about one-third of combat deaths were caused by small-arms fire, while shell fragments accounted for more than one half.[19]

Of course, the damage inflicted by agent orange is ongoing. One didn't have to walk through a sprayed area to be affected, only to drink from a stream or river in its watershed — namely, from any along the heavily populated coastal plain.

(Source: Courtesy of Edward Molina)

Besides "short rounds" and bad water, U.S. servicemen may have endured other unnecessary risks. Just to survive on a modern battle-field, individual soldiers must display a certain amount of skill and initiative. Every time an American private unexpectedly confronts his secretive, enemy counterpart, he must be as good a tactician over 50 yards as his battalion commander is over 3000. He must know how to successfully fire and maneuver through the microterrain. And, if he does so too slowly or predictably, he will be killed. His ability to follow orders and established procedures will not be enough to save him.

(Source: Courtesy of Edward Molina)

7 U.S. Warfare Style in Perspective

- *Does the U.S. use the most moral style of warfare?*
- *Are U.S. infantrymen really the best in the world?*

(Source: FM 22-100 (1983), p. 22)

This Elusive Thing Called Peace

For Americans, war has been unavoidable throughout most of the twentieth century. Adolf Hitler represented an evil that had to be stopped. Joseph Stalin's equally demented record made the Korean intervention and 36 years of intermittently hot Cold War at least understandable. But a conflict's degree of morality depends not only on why it is waged but on how it is waged.

> . . . The hypothesis of legitimate defense, which never concerns an innocent but always and only an unjust aggressor,

must respect the principle that moralists call the *principium inculpatae tutelae* (the principle of nonculpable defense). In order to be legitimate, that "defense" must be carried out in a way that causes the least damage and, if possible, saves the life of the aggressor.[1]
> — Pope John Paul II
> *Crossing the Threshold of Hope*

... [For a defense by military force to be legitimate,] the use of arms must not produce evils and disorders graver than the evil to be eliminated. The power of modern means of destruction weighs very heavily in evaluating this condition.[2]

"Every act of war directed to the indiscriminate destruction of whole cities or vast areas with their inhabitants is a crime against God and man, which merits firm and unequivocal condemnation (GS 80 § 3)." A danger of modern warfare is that it provides the opportunity to those who possess modern scientific weapons — especially atomic, biological, or chemical weapons — to commit such crimes.[3]

Overwhelming Firepower Is Not the Answer

War may be the most obscene of man's inventions. Few who have participated in one have come away unsullied. Ever present is the temptation to intensify the destruction in hopes of curtailing the bloodshed. Despite good intentions, U.S. leaders felt obligated late in WWII to use weapons that overstretched the Geneva Conventions. Because these excesses had occurred gradually and in response to enemy precedents, they were difficult to identify as such. Scores of Japanese population centers had already been incinerated by the time the atomic bombs were dropped. The possibility of moral error became harder to ignore when it was discovered that Nagasaki had been the center of Japanese Christianity.

Americans are just now starting to realize that they could have won WWII with less firepower. There's another (ancient) style of warfare that could have gotten the job done without running afoul of the laws of war. Officially adopted as doctrine by the United States Marine Corps in 1986, it is now called "maneuver" or "common-sense" warfare. Many of its precepts are virtual opposites to those for the traditional "attrition" style. Common-sense tactics depend more on surprise than on firepower. Western military analysts have known about this alternative way of fighting since WWI, but only the Germans have been able to decentralize control enough to use it.

Instead of trying to kill enemy soldiers per se, common-sense leaders bypass and demoralize their opponents whenever possible. Instead of controlling everything from the top, they delegate authority to subordinates. Instead of focusing inward to prevent mistakes, they focus outward on their adversary. They don't choose hilltops as objectives, but more strategically important targets like communication centers, ammunition dumps, or rail heads.

To attack these strategic objectives, common-sense forces seek out gaps in the enemy's defenses and avoid strongpoints. Instead of always using the largest weapon available, they employ smaller weapons in series — one to set up their quarry for the next. They do not move methodically, but with high tempo. They operate through "reconnaissance (recon) pull" instead of "command push." Instead of attacking all along a line in the daytime, they punch a small hole at night and then funnel through it. When surprise has been irreparably compromised, they stop attacking and sometimes back up. They prefer ambush and infiltration to direct confrontation. They defend only to regain momentum, and then often with one or more "fire sacks" or traps.

Of course, there are circumstances in which the methodical or attrition way works better— e.g. while trying to get through the defensive barbed wire surrounding a prepared enemy position. But, usually, the common-sense option contributes more to winning the war and limiting casualties. Ground forces must be able to shift easily between the two opposing styles as circumstances dictate. Many of the world's largest armies have at one time or another in their history already demonstrated this capability: i.e. the Germans, Russians, Japanese, Chinese, North Koreans, and North Vietnamese.

The Individual and Small Unit Must Be Better Prepared

Since WWI, the highest priority in this country has been the winning of battles at minimal cost. One wonders why this goal hasn't been realized in the casualty statistics. Purportedly to save lives, Americans have routinely insisted on the most technologically advanced equipment. Most of the hard-to-acquire training dollars go toward teaching U.S. military personnel how to use the latest models. To survive in combat, a U.S. soldier must know more than just how to use his equipment.

To avert friendly casualties, American forces have also tried to conduct battles from long range — so much so that their short-range-warfighting capabilities have severely deteriorated. Becoming proficient at close combat requires carefully training and then trusting enlisted small-unit leaders — something that armies modeled after the French and British have great difficulty doing. Where rank is glorified, commissioned college graduates are expected to know more about small-unit combat after six months of classroom instruction than career enlisted men know after many years of practical experience. Corporate managers have no trouble seeing the flaw in this type of reasoning. Collectively, those who practice small-unit tactics will usually know more about that particular subject than their commanders or higher headquarters. To become proficient at close combat, infantry organizations may have to allow subunits to identify and correct their own tactical deficiencies — to generate their own training from the bottom up.

⑧ The Winds of Change

● *When does the attacker have the edge?*

● *In which ways are U.S. infantry units deficient?*

(Source: FM 22-100 (1983), p. 30)

He Who Can't Learn from History Is Doomed to Repeat It

Too much emphasis on high-level coordination and long-range warfare is bound to produce shortfalls in other areas. Those under constant pressure to utilize new equipment might be tempted to discount small-unit and individual skills. For example, commanders with electronic location finders might see less need for subordinates who can land navigate through terrain association. In combat, electronic gadgets have less survivability than individual skills. On Tarawa, a device that had been under refinement for over 40 years failed miserably.

The situation was compounded by a near-total loss of communication by the landing force. The command nets on the flagship . . . failed with the first crashing salvos of the main batteries 3 hours prior to H-hour. The fragile TBX troop radios, totally susceptible to water, failed at almost every hand.[1]

— *Marine Corps Gazette* (November 1993)

To discover which close-combat techniques may not have not made it into the institutional knowledge of the U.S. military, one must look at the history of small-unit tactics worldwide. While tactics can't be done by formula per se, what happens at the squad level and below has remained relatively constant since WWI. From casualty comparisons, one can see unmistakable trends in the relative risk of what lower echelons attempt or are ordered to do. As a result, military historians generally agree on several axioms of logic (or common sense) with which to limit casualties. U.S. commanders have not only been slow to follow these axioms, but also quick to impugn adversaries who do. To fully appreciate what happens in combat at the squad level, all but those who have been there must call on their imaginations.

What a Rifle Squad Member Must Know to Survive

Pretend to be one of the hundreds of U.S. infantrymen making the final "push" through the Hurtgen Forest toward the German Westwall in the recent movie *When Trumpets Fade*.[2] Everyone's on line and walking east. Suddenly, someone steps on a mine, and the entire unit finds itself under a preregistered enemy artillery barrage. While this type of attack is typical of U.S. forces, it's very costly against anyone who knows what they're doing. Here's why.

"Prepared enemy positions" are those for which fighting holes have been dug, antipersonnel barriers enhanced, interlocking machinegun fire arranged, and dead space covered by mines or indirect fire. "Deliberate attacks" are those preceded by reconnaissance and rehearsal. Because "hastily attacking" a prepared enemy position generates little surprise, it normally produces too many casualties. Unfortunately, most U.S. infantry attacks have been of the hasty variety. The first few minutes of the film *Saving Private Ryan*[3] have been replayed on almost every battlefield since 1917, whether near a beach or not. Meanwhile, most attacks by opposing forces — the Japanese,[4] Germans,[5] and North Vietnamese,[6] for example — have been meticulously planned and therefore decidedly deliberate. That's why enemy soldiers have been accused of not thinking as well on their feet as Americans. The truth of the matter is that no one thinks well on their feet after (1) becoming convinced that there is only one way to do things, (2) two hours of sleep a night for months on end, and (3) shells bursting all around them. What to do in battle has to be brainstormed and rehearsed ahead of time.

Occasionally, small opposition forces — like the German stormtrooper squads of WWI — have attained enough proficiency to "transcend technique." They have punched their way through successive lines of defense without much advance reconnaissance. But one should not confuse these decidedly quicker deliberate attacks with the hasty variety. The German squads had carefully rehearsed how changing circumstance might alter their techniques and were using recon pull to identify those circumstances.

Why are opponent strengths from past wars just now being recognized as such? One reason is the recent declassification of several U.S. War Department studies. Of course, few American commanders will openly admit to having run hasty attacks against prepared enemy positions. In their minds, those attacks were all satisfactorily reconnoitered and rehearsed. But remember, they are thinking in terms of battalion- or company-sized maneuver elements. A Japanese, German, or North Vietnamese officer thinks in terms of platoon- or squad-sized maneuver elements. Both categories of commander can attack with a large unit, but the Easterner punches a hole with a squad or platoon first. The American commander reconnoiters his objective with map study, aerial reconnaissance, and binocular assessment. His Eastern counterpart dispatches infiltrators not only to map his objective from the inside, but also to keep its occupants under close surveillance. The difference is in the amount of detail in the intelligence gathered. Knowing where every defender's weapon is located ahead of time opens up a whole new world of tactical opportunity. WWII Russians continually reconnoitered ahead of attacks through urban terrain,[7] something that most Western tacticians would never consider. As in the movie *Platoon,*[8] U.S. commanders liken stumbling onto well hidden enemy bunkers to getting ambushed. This may not appear to be a problem, but it is. To "rescue" buddies caught in the kill zone, American infantrymen are taught to instinctively assault through ambushers within 50 yards of themselves. Against bunkers, this constitutes hastily attacking a prepared enemy position.

On the matter of pre-attack rehearsal, again many U.S. commanders have a different definition than their Eastern counterparts. To some Americans, simply talking about what to do, qualifies. For others, unit familiarity with standard operating procedures and doctrinal methods makes additional rehearsal superfluous. When soldiers must cooperate well to succeed against a prepared enemy position, rehearsing as completely as in the film *The Dirty Dozen*[9] produces a more satisfactory result.

In the U.S. Armed Forces, the problem has been one of over-controlled operations and training. Units have had neither the leeway to correct tactical deficiencies in peacetime nor to capitalize on local opportunities in war. When platoons are little more than dots on a regimental commander's grease pencil board, squads end up rushing enemy machineguns. Because a single machinegun can stop almost any ground attack (one section decimated two British battalions at the Somme),[10] enemy objectives must be assaulted silently or with weapons that sound like indirect fire or mines. In other words, at the squad level, U.S. infantry forces have been forced to practice what amounts to premachinegun tactics. Other armies have managed to avoid this cruel by-product of overcontrol. Throughout WWII, Russian and Japanese soldiers were told *not* to shoot their small arms during night assaults. Thirty years later, NVA soldiers were told the same thing.

> For a night attack (attack in smoke) the moment of surprise must be utilized to the fullest extent to destroy the enemy. Under conditions of total silence the squad quickly approaches the enemy, attacks him without opening fire and without battle cries and destroys him with bayonets or hand grenades.[11]
>
> — "Soviet Infantry Tactics in World War II"
> from *Soviet Combat Regulations of 1942*

The infantry assault [during the night attack] is with the bayonet without firing.[12]
— TM-E 30-480
Handbook on Japanese Military Forces

Success in the [NVA] attack is dependent on being able to breach the perimeter undetected. The assault is violent and invariably from more than one direction. It begins with a preparation, usually mortar and RPG fires. . . . Small arms are not employed except to cover the withdrawal in order to avoid disclosing the location of attacking forces. Once defending troops are forced into the bunkers, penetration of the perimeter is effected. Mortars cease firing, but the illusion of incoming fire is maintained through the use of RPG's, grenades, and satchel charges.[13]
— *NVA-VC Small Unit Tactics & Techniques Study*
U.S. Department of Defense

How Important Is Terrain to Tactics?

Contrary to popular opinion, only in urban terrain does the defender have the edge. In the city, even a technologically disadvantaged defender can prevail. Jews armed with squirrel rifles and molotov cocktails stopped an entire German army at Warsaw — twice. Only by flooding and razing the ghetto did Hitler's henchmen ever clear it.

By January [of 1942], when the fighters had their first baptism of fire, they had a store of 143 revolvers, one machine pistol and seven rounds of ammunition per weapon. . . . Their numbers increased to six hundred and fifty, divided into 22 groups. . . . The Ghetto fighters constructed an intricate network of underground cellars and tunnels. Concealed retreats and passages for shifting and distributing the defense forces were also devised. . . .
. . . A hail of bullets, grenades, and bombs poured down on the Germans. . . . Tanks were brought in but the fighters aimed a barrage of gasoline-filled bottles. . . . The Germans

quickly realized the Ghetto could not be cleared in one burst of action. . . . At noon the Germans dammed up the sewers and flooded them. . . . Only fire could destroy the Ghetto. Stroop then decided to destroy the entire residential area by setting every block on fire.[14]

In rural terrain, the defender is at a disadvantage. If an attacker with the proper prerehearsed techniques can get close enough to a prepared enemy position undetected, he can invariably punch his way into it. Single stormtrooper squads routinely penetrated U.S. lines late in WWI. The Huns could easily expand their newly captured sections of trench, because Doughboys at other locations heard only grenade explosions and thought them to be part of the indirect-fire attack. Technique is everything.

The essential elements of the tactics that [German Captain] Rohr developed in the course of these experiments were (1) the replacement of the advance in skirmish lines with the surprise assault of squad-sized "stormtroops," (2) the use of supporting arms . . . coordinated at the lowest possible level . . . to suppress the enemy during the attack, and (3) the clearing of trenches by rolling them up with troops armed with hand grenades.[15]

In fact, only by completely surprising the opposition can a rural defender consistently succeed. Before reaching a static main line of resistance, the attacking unit must be forced to deploy early or at least have its momentum interrupted. Squad-sized security patrols and ambushes, for the most part, provide this service. Otherwise enemy subunits can approach their objective along different routes and then rendezvous just outside friendly lines. Once they do, their lead element can almost always get in. If defensive battles for rural terrain are won forward of friendly lines, then what happens forward of those lines becomes crucial. With proper techniques, a single two-man listening post can make an attacker of any size pause to reconsider. Picture Privates Campbell and Sobkowiak in a well concealed position just off the enemy's main avenue of approach. They have been allowed to preregister their own artillery target and deploy a command-detonated string of claymore mines. When the enemy force (however big) shows up, those two privates can pretty well interrupt its momentum without ever disclosing their own presence. For the stationary defender, not using patrols and outposts to engage his attacker early can spell disaster.

With obstacle networks, hidden positions, tunneling, and ditching, Eastern armies have given rural terrain the defensive attributes of an urban area. Additionally, the Japanese,[16] Germans,[17] and Russians,[18] have all made extensive use of subunit perimeters and dummy positions at the main line of resistance. Many an unwary opponent has ended up assaulting an unoccupied portion of those "lines" and then being cut to shreds by machinegun fire from both flanks. These subunit perimeters are highly reminiscent of the mutually supporting yet semi-independent squad-sized strongpoints with which the Germans replaced continuously manned front lines late in WWI.

When attacking through rural terrain, the contemporary maneuver element still has to exercise a good deal of caution. If it is detected in the envelopment route, no amount of cover fire can save it — one enemy MK-19 (automatic grenade thrower) or fuel air explosive can stop it cold. Just to weather old-fashioned machinegun fire, the assault element must deceive the quarry as to the reason for smoke and explosions in his wire. Assaulting with minimal losses takes deception, stealth, and speed. Because the determined defender need not expose any vital organ to do his job, no amount of suppressive fire can take the place of surprise.

WHAT U.S. INFANTRY SQUADS PRESENTLY KNOW

If the reader were to ask a squad of American infantrymen to describe their techniques for moving across a street under fire, they would say, "It depends on the situation," or "We'll do whatever the platoon leader directs." Essentially, they don't have any street-crossing techniques — the manuals only generally describe urban combat. In a way, that's a blessing. Becoming convinced that the one way in the book will work under any circumstance can be detrimental to one's health. However, crossing a street under fire is an example of storming a prepared enemy position — it can't be done safely without a deliberate attack. That means the assault must be rehearsed and the objective reconnoitered. Marines supported by tanks took three days to cross a single street during the battle for Hue City.[19] Waiting for one's foe to appear before planning an attack gives that foe an additional advantage. Like a football team, the U.S. squad needs several prerehearsed "plays" for crossing streets and then quickly to ascertain defender alignment before running the most appropriate play. To attain the requisite level of surprise, those plays must incorporate deception, shock, and speed.

If asked how to counter an enemy ambush, most of the members of that same U.S. squad would probably say, "Run an immediate action drill" — one of several stand-up assaults described in the manuals. They naturally assume that the manuals contain the latest product of organizational research. They've been told that ambushes happen so quickly that they can only be countered by an instinctive (devoid of thinking) reaction. Again, this is an attack against what often amounts to a prepared enemy position; assaulting upright is not the answer. The squad needs different options. As soon as its members get ambushed, they should normally get down — to create the deception that everyone has been hit and give those outside the kill zone a chance to change location without being seen. After those in the maneuver element crawl out of sight, they can quickly confer on who's in charge and which counterattack technique to run.

Why is this cornerstone of the world's greatest defense establishment coming up with impractical answers? Is it because squad members are incapable of doing any better without the advice of college-trained leaders? Or is it because they've been overcontrolled to the extent that their God-given thought processes have been successfully suppressed? In a micromanaged unit, any creative thinking or questioning from lower echelons is perceived as disruptive.

In essence, every U.S. soldier must learn to defend him or herself against any threat — including tank or NBC attack. Because there are no front lines in modern war, this requirement applies equally to combat, combat-support, and combat-service-support personnel. The only way in which the last two differ from the first is that they generally guard strategic targets and have less wherewithal with which to do it. Those who served in the "rear areas" of Vietnam remember all too well the patter of little feet and subsequent explosions.

Part Three

For Those Who Still Serve

If you would win a man to your cause, first convince him that you are his sincere friend. Therein is a drop of honey that catches his heart, which, say what he will, is the great high road to his reason and which, once gained, you will find but little trouble in convincing his judgment of the justice of your cause, if indeed that cause be a just one. On the contrary, assume to dictate to his judgment, or to command his action, or to mark him as one to be shunned and despised and he will retreat within himself, close all avenues to his head and his heart. . . . Such is man, and so must he be understood by those who would lead him, even to his own best interest.
— Abraham Lincoln

A Job for the Tactical Technicians

- *Who in industry develops manufacturing methods?*
- *Who should design individual through squad tactics?*

(Source: FM 22-100 (1983), p. 274)

Who Really Wins the Wars?

Were WWI, WWII, and the Korean War really won by the generals and colonels, as the newspapers and history books would have Americans believe? Millions of lower ranking veterans share a somewhat different view. There is ample evidence to suggest that many of the individual and small-unit engagements were won, not because of what headquarters had directed, but in spite of it.

If there is a shortfall in close-combat skills in the U.S. infantry, then the lowest echelons of that organization must be called on to fix it. For the most part, commanders and their staff officers have little personal experience with close combat. It is subunits controlled by sergeants and corporals that make the actual contact with aggressors during training. What many Americans may not realize is that the proud heritage of the U.S. infantry is largely the product of NCO initiative. To fully appreciate this, one must take another walk through yesteryear.

Pride and courage have always defined the U.S. infantryman. But, as enemy weapons systems have changed, so have the ways he can safely display those characteristics on the battlefield. In the days of smoothbore weaponry, he and his buddies could move by the quickest route possible to a location 50 meters or so from their opponents and then assault en mass. As barrels became rifled, defenders had to be approached more carefully. Fully exposed Union forces made no fewer than fourteen futile assaults on Marye's Heights at Fredericksburg.[1] Then, with the invention of the machinegun, warfare changed forever. Since WWI, most battles have been decided by small groups of men silencing enemy machineguns, e.g. those led by Marine Medal of Honor recipients Sergeant Kocak and Gunnery Sergeant Cukela in WWI and Corporal Stein in WWII. But pride and courage can't outsmart a bullet, only common sense can do that.

To determine how much of a contribution NCO's may have made, one must analyze where American infantrymen learned what they know about tactics. As latecomers to WWI, U.S. forces made a terrible mistake by accepting training from the British and French — both of whom had long overemphasized rank. British offensive skill had been demonstrated at the Somme, where, after a preparatory fire of two million shells, 100,000 British infantrymen "went over the top" in the early summer of 1916. At the end of the first day, they had acquired 60,000 casualties and one quarter of the first German trench.[2] French soldiers, on the other hand, had been forced to use attrition tactics against German machineguns since 1915. When they finally objected, their commanding general discontinued offensive operations and tightened control. The French military had opted for centralized control and glorification of rank over tactical innovation, and this set the stage for what was to become a tragic military history.

When U.S. Marines reached the Pacific in early 1942, they discovered a very sophisticated opponent. The enemy had new tactics and more training. Some estimates have Japanese privates receiving up to one year of night attack training. The Marines who faced them had a choice — either to learn quickly or die. What those Marines had to learn the hard way got shared in countless conversations aboard Navy transports, in foxholes, or on liberty through what has come to be known as the "NCO chain of command." While the generalship was good in those years, what turned the tide in the Pacific was an NCO Corps strong enough to disseminate lessons learned.

More recently, the Marines tackled an equally skilled opponent in Vietnam. During the longest war in U.S. history, Marine NCO's were expected to take over when their commanders got wounded, yet had no formal training in tactical decision making. Prior to 1973, Marine company commanders relied on their NCO's to do most of the leading, training, and making of personnel assignments. Then, to overcome some disciplinary problems in the Corps, its officers usurped those traditional NCO functions. For example, the rifle company executive officer took over the training. (To this day, the Marine company/platoon tactics manual names the company gunnery sergeant as the commander's representative for training.[3]) Instead of blaming the NCO's, Marine officers should have looked into what effect losing a war with inferior infantry tactics might have had on morale.

Headquarters Can Only Do So Much

All Marines are now and always have been considered infantrymen. As there are no front lines in modern war, this is one of their finest qualities. Yet, in organizations as with individuals, stated objectives mean little without commensurate action. For bootcamp graduates going to infantry units, entry-level training has been cut from three months to four weeks — barely enough time to learn how to shoot the crew-served weapons. Disturbingly, most U.S. Army combat-service-support personnel see themselves as noncombatants. In many Army units, NCO's are allowed even less initiative than their Marine brethren.

What will be required to move forward? U.S. infantrymen cannot allow a zero-defect environment and exaggerated technology claims to keep them from improving individual and small-unit skills. They can't continue to treat only the symptoms of an underlying tactical deficiency.

By designing and conducting individual through squad training, NCO's could practice tactical decision making while improving their parent organization's warfighting methods. Those NCO's are (1) the tactical technicians of any unit, (2) the leaders directly in contact with the enemy, and (3) the members best qualified to determine how riflemen, buddy teams, fire teams, and squads can best operate in war. Contained in each period of instruction is normally one way to accomplish a composite task of some combat mission. This way is called a "technique." By requiring an instructor to measure the surprise or casualties generated by each technique he teaches, and then to improve on that technique, his commander forces him to choose between tactical options. Organizational knowledge on individual and small-unit tactical technique is best served by dynamic learning — encouraging every NCO to find new ways to accomplish assigned tasks with fewer casualties (or more surprise) and then to share their discoveries with one another.

> My many years in the Army have demonstrated that wherever confidence in NCO's is lacking . . . you have . . . no really combat-worthy units.[4]
> — Georgi K. Zhukov
>   victor of Stalingrad and Berlin

10 A Different View of the World

- *Does freely expending ordnance save U.S. lives?*
- *Are infantrymen taught what they need to survive?*

(Source: FM 90-6 (1980), p. C-4)

The Shift Away from Attrition Warfare Is Long Overdue

Attrition warfare has become as much a part of Americana as Mom's apple pie. For a number of socio-economic reasons, among them the acquisition of power and money, the West has gravitated toward it — tried to solve all of its problems with tight control and new weapons. While the Germans were developing squad tactics to counter the machinegun, the Western Allies were inventing the tank. But space age helmets with computer imaging of friendly locations can't replace individual and small-unit skills. With normal vision partially obstructed by a computer module, U.S. soldiers worry that a helmet-mounted TV camera might be next. Control from behind the lines can never replace freedom to react to immediate circumstances. Technology didn't turn the tables in Vietnam, nor in the more recent "War on Drugs." Nor will it work in any vegetated or uneven terrain. What the arms and target acquisition sellers have failed to mention is that most potential adversaries like to operate below ground and camouflage themselves. Radar will not pick them up. Riflemen will have no one to target with their infrared dots. So many engagements will occur at once, that no amount of supporting arms will be sufficient.

Common-Sense Warfare Is More Efficient and Moral

While common-sense (maneuver) warfare has been officially Marine Corps doctrine since 1986, its assimilation has been only partial because of delays in overhauling organizational procedures. While its use at the task force level produced a quick and relatively bloodless victory in the Gulf, it has yet to be adopted at squad level because of headquarters' reluctance to decentralize control over operations or training. This alternative way of fighting focuses on strategic targets and therefore does more to further the war effort than its predecessor. It also kills fewer people — friendly, enemy, and civilian. By bypassing enemy strongpoints and using less ordnance, units loose fewer personnel to enemy machineguns and friendly artillery. Civilians must endure less crossfire.

Other armies have known the advantages of this alternative way of fighting for decades. The NVA needed no tanks or planes to defeat the U.S. military in Vietnam. The North Koreans passed through South Korea like a ghost — leaving almost everything intact. To evict the Chinese from Korea, the U.S. 8th Army resorted to leveling everything in its path. In WWII, any use of flame — whether by flamethrower, flame tank, and or incendiary bomb — stretched existing Geneva Conventions. The destruction of noncombatant population centers violated all established laws of war.

Basically, attrition warfare discounts the value of both friendly and opposition soldier/civilian. A rifle range mentality — "all ready on the right, all ready on the left, all ready on the firing line" — only saves lives in training. In combat, it gives the enemy more time to prepare. Then, while U.S. soldiers avoid shooting each other in the back, enemy machineguns kill them by the hundreds. The Eastern style of war (devoid of political subversion) allows more moral options. It also minimizes losses from enemy machinegun fire.

A number of political pressures have made it difficult to fully embrace this alternative method. Less firing does little to help next year's budget or the economy in general. Dispersion of troops takes decentralized control — something that grates against time-honored procedure, mistake avoidance, and rank consciousness.

The Transition Has Been Only Partially Realized

Tactics are situational. Good tactics are those that get the job done at least cost. Though attrition and common-sense warfare styles are largely opposite,[1] either will work under the right circumstances. Unfortunately, military organizations promote traditional ways of doing things. It's hard for military men to accept that what they've always heard isn't always the best way.

Attrition War	Common-Sense War
Tries to Kill Enemy	Tries to Bypass/Demoralize Foe
Depends On Firepower	Depends On Surprise
Takes Central Control	Takes Decentralized Control
Focus Is Inward on Self	Focus is Outward on Enemy
Hits Concentrations	Moves through Gaps
Objectives Are Hilltops	Objs. Are "Centers of Gravity"
Biggest Weapon Used	Combined Arms Employed
Methodical	High Tempo
Command Push	Reconnaissance Pull
Attacks All Along a Line	Exploits Breakthroughs
Day Attacks Only	Mostly Night Attacks
Never Retreats	Sometimes Backs Up
Defends Often	Defends Only As a Trap
War Takes a Long Time	War Won Quickly

Table 10.1: The Two Warfare Styles Are Opposites

The looser control parameters of common-sense warfare make many commanders nervous. They must realize that each subordinate's degree of initiative will be proportional to his freedom of action. Much of their combat control will be accomplished during training. Once the battle starts, instead of asking for instructions, subunit leaders will submit after-action reports.

Attrition Style	Common-Sense Style
All Do What Told	Initiative Encouraged
Unit Asks Permission	Unit Informs Commander
Detailed Orders	Mission Type Orders
Control through Orders	Control through Training
Train to a Standard	Train As They Want
Train As Always	Train to the Threat
Complicated Signaling	Not Much Signaling Necessary

Table 10.2: Different Control Parameters

What a single squad trained in common-sense warfare can accomplish over the last hundred yards is truly amazing.[2] What keeps it safe is that the enemy doesn't know it's there.

— Find/disrupt a larger enemy force before it can attack.
— Handle a much bigger opponent in a chance encounter.
— Extricate itself intact from an enemy ambush.
— Ambush, with little risk, an enemy force of any size.
— Perform short-range infiltration of enemy lines.
— Single-handedly force a gap in enemy lines at night.
— Single-handedly force a gap in those lines in the day.
— Defend against infiltrator, tank, and NBC attacks.
— From successive fall-back positions, defend a city block.
— Clear one side of a street faster than foe thinks possible.

Table 10.3: What A Common-Sense Squad Can Do

11 Preserving Limited Assets in Wartime

● *How hard is it to stop well trained sappers?*
● *What does it take to stop an enemy ground attack?*

(Sources: FM 21-76 (1957), pp. 55, 57)

Other Nations Have Had to Work Harder to Preserve Assets

While Christianity puts a high value on human life per se, its principles are difficult to practice in a materialistic, Western society. Certain forms of civilized behavior occur more often and are better rewarded by many Eastern cultures. There, people must work together ("gung ho" in Chinese), possibly because they lack the infrastructure to coexist any other way. Patience is highly prized throughout the Orient. Nonviolence and fasting (from any excess) have become so deeply ingrained in the Indian lifestyle that a young girl can still safely wander the streets of Calcutta after dark.

Whatever harm an enemy may do to any enemy, or a hater
to a hater, an ill-directed mind inflicts on oneself a greater
harm.[1]
    — inscription from ruins at Sarnath
    where Buddha first preached

Certainly, most Eastern nations enjoy less means with which to
make war. They've had to try harder to preserve limited assets.
Whether one saves lives to preserve assets or to uphold religious
beliefs, the end result is the same. Part of what these more ancient,
Eastern societies have discovered is how to get the same military
mission accomplished with fewer personnel. When fewer people
are involved, fewer people are endangered.

The IJA [Imperial Japanese Army] founded its battle doctrine on bold offensive operations. . . . The IJA relied on the
infantry as its main battle force. . . . [T]acticians had to guar-
antee that the attacking Japanese infantry reached the enemy positions with a minimum of friendly losses.[2]
    — Leavenworth Papers No. 2

By 1920 IJA tacticians realized the need to disperse infantry formations in order to reduce losses when attacking a
defender who possessed the lethal firepower of modern weapons. The revised 1925 edition of the Infantry Manual emphasized tactics designed to allow the attacker to reach the
enemy defender's position.[3]

 . . . These [tactics] included infantry cooperation with
other combat arms, . . . night fighting and maneuver, . . .
increased reliance on the independent decision-making ability of junior officers and *non-commissioned officers* [italics
added]. . . .
 By the 1930's, IJA planners realized more than ever that
the Japanese army could not fight a war of attrition against
the ever growing might of the Soviet Union. Consequently,
they designed and refined their tactics to wage a short war
fought to a quick and decisive conclusion.[4]
    — Leavenworth Papers No. 2

Piecing Together How to Work Smarter from History

What has happened in war doesn't change, but how it is perceived does — as the thought processes of past adversaries are better understood. Only recently, have former U.S. commanders begun to grasp how effectively the paradoxical, highly deceptive, Oriental or common-sense style of war has been used against them. By closely examining similar episodes from different conflicts, one can actually discover how to practice this alternative way of fighting at the small-unit level. In modern combat, infantry units should be able to force their way into an enemy strongpoint with a single squad. (While the specifics of this maneuver are well known to most potential antagonists, they deserve limited distribution and will not be discussed here.) Combat- and combat-service-support units must be able to defend themselves against any threat. How this is accomplished can be explained and should give Americans some idea of enemy ground attack capabilities. For the defender, the principal threats to his position come from short-range infiltrators (sappers), enemy assault troops, or tanks.

Stopping Sappers

A sapper attack is one in which small groups of men sneak through a defender's lines to conduct some subsequent operation. To understand how effective this type of attack can be, one must first ponder the meaning of several disjointed stories from Vietnam.

Vietnam

After seeing what appeared to be someone wriggling through the protective wire just before dawn at Dong Ha in September of 1966, a Marine lieutenant left the perimeter to look for footprints. On finding none, he headed back in. Then, on an impulse, he spun around in his tracks. What he saw that morning would become an important milestone in his military education. No further than 50 yards away was a black figure, carrying no visible equipment, who proceeded to scamper behind a six-foot hillock sparsely covered with small bushes. The lieutenant pulled out his pistol and walked to where the figure had disappeared. After stomping across every inch of ground and pulling on every bush for over 30 minutes, he returned to his perimeter too embarrassed to tell anyone of his encounter.[5] If an enemy soldier can live within 100 yards of a major U.S. installation and leave his hole to relieve himself each morning, one has to wonder how he spends his evenings.

(Source: FM 6-13E1/2 (1979), p. 2-359)

In January of 1969, a Marine company was tasked with guarding the An Hoa ammunition dump for one night and then allowed to return to the field. At 7 A.M. the following day, from a distance of 15,000 meters, its members witnessed a mushroom-shaped cloud rise from where the ammunition had been. The story told at the time was that (1) the dump had been hit by a lucky mortar round, (2) no remains of any defender recovered, (3) the end of the base bulldozed, and (4) new protective wire laid.[6]

Later that month, rumor had it that eight helicopters had been hit by a lucky string of mortar rounds at the Marble Mountain Air Wing Facility.[7] After the war, it was discovered that the VC had been using the caves under this particular mountain as a staging area for years.

It would appear that Viet Cong sappers did more to further the Communist war effort than U.S. commanders realized. For most, the error was not one of integrity, but rather of trying to understand common-sense tactics through attrition warfare eyes. A few more short stories may shed some light on what really happened at Guadalcanal.

Guadalcanal

Historians generally agree that enemy soldiers appeared inside the Henderson Field perimeter on numerous occasions. Still a matter of speculation is what they all were doing there. General Vandegrift's Chief of Staff estimated that hundreds of Japanese had gotten through friendly lines, but saw no incongruity in only one Marine being killed by a sniper.[8]

While Edson's Raiders were making their famous Bloody Ridge "stand" in mid-September of 1942, Sheffield Banta was evicting enemy sappers from the Division Command Post (almost a mile behind the lines).[9]

Some Japanese actually reached Henderson Field. Four, led by an officer brandishing a *samurai* sword, broke into the Division CP. . . .

Shrieking *"banzai!"* the quartet fell upon the CP staff. Startled Marines opened fire with their pistols and carbines. The infiltrators dropped dead at their feet, but not until the [Japanese] officer had killed a sergeant with his sword.[10]

. . . Small groups of enemy that have infiltrated may appear any place. On Guadalcanal a three-man enemy patrol attacked the First Marine Division CP.[11]
— FMFRP 12-9
Jungle Warfare

Infiltrators also damaged strategic targets inside the perimeter in less obvious ways. Some were supporting-arms forward observers. NCO's told Chesty Puller of intruders using radios and rifle shots as signals.[12] On 13 October, Pistol Pete (enemy long-range artillery) was "registered . . . with slow and methodical precision."[13] But too much precision can mean concurrent sabotage. The airfield had come under aerial or naval bombardment almost every day and night (often at predictable hours). Well dispersed and revetted aircraft, ammunition, and fuel had routinely fallen victim to these attacks. After American sentries dove for cover, CP's, equipment, and stores would have been easier to approach along the ground. Could Japanese sappers have been responsible for some of the direct hits?

On the night of October 14th [actually October 13-14], a Japanese naval task force, including the mighty battleships *Kongo* and *Haruna,* swung into "Sleepless Lagoon" off Henderson Field and began firing salvos. At short range, the big 14-inch shells hit accurately, ripped up the runway, smashed planes, killed and mangled marines, and set gasoline stores and ammunition dumps into roaring flames. For an hour and twenty minutes the shelling went on while the marines prayed or cursed. Then the Japanese ships withdrew, leaving more than half of the ninety planes on the airfield wrecked, the gasoline supply almost all destroyed.[14]
— Richard Tregaskis
news correspondent on Guadalcanal

Tons of fourteen- and twelve-inch shells began to land in and around the Division CP [over a mile from Henderson Field].[15]

— 1st Division Operations Officer on Guadalcanal

Kongo and *Haruna* and their cruiser and destroyer escorts used the last of their ammunition at 0230, and left the channel. . . .

Before anyone in the Perimeter could organize damage-control parties, a chain of Japanese night bombers arrived to make matters worse. A direct hit on Texas Switch, the garrison's main radio station, prevented word of the disaster from going out until nearly dawn. . . .

Archer Vandegrift arrived at Air Ops to find a dejected Roy Geiger viewing the wreckage of his headquarters building.[16]

. . . In twenty-four hours on October 13 and 14, [only] fifty-three bombs and shells hit the [mile-long] Henderson airstrip! . . .

Private 1st Class Warner Pyne, P Battery, 5th Battalion, 11th Marines . . . was in the command post when the shelling began, but . . . scrambled to another hole about half a mile away. . . . During the night that command post took a direct hit, killing everyone who had remained there.[17]

The evidence is there, albeit circumstantial. Even for closely observed fire, the limits of probability have been exceeded by this many direct hits on pinpoint targets. One can conclude that enemy sappers — with satchel charges, timers, and supporting-arms deceptions — have been covertly blowing up U.S. war materiel since 1942. Wars are won by destroying strategic targets (not people), and sappers can get the job done more efficiently and safely.

The key to stopping sappers is proper fighting-hole placement and fields-of-fire clearance. To have much of a chance, each defender must have (1) grazing fire out to beyond grenade range to his front, and (2) level, unobstructed ground out to neighboring positions on his flanks. Further, his exact location must be kept secret. That often means shifting positions after dark, preparing perfect camouflage, and never silhouetting oneself. All this will go for naught if U.S. leaders continue to walk the lines. The vigilance of subordinates can be monitored by tugrope.

Averting a Ground Infantry Assault

In this type of attack, the enemy maneuver element forces its way through the defender's lines. Here's a thought to ponder — if destroying a pinpoint strategic target is the goal, how big does the attacking force have to be? A second set of stories from Vietnam reveals another way U.S. forces have been beaten without realizing it.

Vietnam

In the Spring of 1968, the regimental headquarters company commander was walking through a dimly lit billeting area inside the 27th Marines compound south of Da Nang. He came upon an agitated roommate who had just bumped into a black figure. The intruder had run between the tents, clotheslined himself on somebody's wash, and then disappeared. The regimental commander was immediately told of the sighting, but wisely decided not to look for the culprit.[18] Why throw an entire camp into turmoil looking for someone who can move unobserved across flat and unobstructed ground, through three rows of protective barbed wire, and between wide-awake sentries?

Throughout the Vietnam war, detailed maps of major U.S. installations were discovered on recently captured enemy soldiers. Local barbers usually took the blame, because a few had been seen pacing off their compounds. Unfortunately, many of these maps were of bases devoid of indigenous workers.

During the never-ending "search and destroy" sweeps in Vietnam, rifle companies occasionally stumbled upon buried ammunition, weapons, rice, and medical caches. These discoveries were usually preceded by a brief firefight or the sight of discarded U.S. gear (signifying a past firefight).[19]

One evening in the late summer of 1968, at a small Marine

outpost just south of Liberty Bridge (where the road between An Hoa and Hill 55 crosses the Song Thu Bon River), the commanders of a rifle company and artillery battery were taking turns looking southeast through a huge set of binoculars called a "B.C. Scope." At a range of several thousand meters, they spotted in the patchwork of rice paddies and forest what appeared to be a single file of 40 running bushes. As the enemy unit approached a woods that would finally obscure them from view, the observers had to make a difficult decision — whether to shoot without clearance or let the target get away. Asking for clearance would have given their quarry 20 minutes to move unobserved in an uncertain direction.[20]

These stories contain all the major elements of the enemy's infantry assault methodology. An NVA (or main-force VC) unit wishing to force its way into an American base approached it through long-range infiltration (subordinate elements used different routes and then reassembled). Its heavy gear had been pre-staged along those routes, so that the elements could transit free-fire zones (for 15 miles or more) quickly. The local VC played a larger role in these assaults than has been publicly acknowledged. In short, they handled all local security and reconnaissance.[21] That means they (1) reconnoitered the objectives (often from the inside), (2) guarded infiltration routes and supply caches, (3) followed U.S. ambushers into position to mark occupied trails, and finally (4) guided attackers through the obstacles surrounding their final objective (mines, barbed wire, early warning devices, etc.).

The Viet Cong [or NVA] fighting method was characterized as "one slow, four quick." The slow was all the painstaking preparation that they put into any operation: repeated reconnaissance of the target, the building of a scale model of the objective so that the men assigned to the mission would recognize every feature, rehearsals of the planned attack as part of training, and the placing of arms caches and food dumps in forward areas. The four "quicks" followed when the operation actually began. First, there was the movement from the base area to the region of the objective, usually in small groups that would only reassemble just before they were to go into action. Then came the attack itself, where speed was the essence. The third "quick" was the clearance of vital arms from the battlefield and the retrieval of the dead and wounded. Finally, there was withdrawal. This was always scrupulously prepared as part of the original plan and depended heavily on a detailed knowledge of the local terrain and the position of enemy forces. . . .

An incoming intelligence report was the start of most main-force Viet Cong [or NVA] operations. The usual source of intelligence was the local guerrillas, Viet Cong part-timers who worked the land for a living but took time off to plant booby traps, carry out raids on weakly defended targets or reconnoitre US firebases and LZs. Reports would come in to the headquarters of a main-force Viet Cong [or NVA] regiment, indicating a number of potential targets. If the regimental commander liked the sound of one of these, he would send out some of his own reconnaissance personnel to contact the Viet Cong villagers and be taken on a guided tour of the objective. Then, if everything seemed right — the avenues of approach, assault and withdrawal all good — the operation would be authorized, a unit assigned and detailed planning begun.

Soon every man in the chosen [main-force] Viet Cong [or NVA] unit would know the target like the back of his hand — every defensive installation, building, fuel store, weapon emplacement. And he would know exactly what he personally had to do, the route of advance, his part in the assault, the assembly point after the fight and the various routes back to base. . . .

The objective would often be several days march from the [main-force] Viet Cong [or NVA] base in the Highlands, or across the border from Laos or Cambodia. To remain unobserved during this advance was essential. The small columns of men would thread their way silently through the jungle, dropping to the ground at the sound of an aircraft. They carried twigs and leaves attached to wire frames on their backs that provided perfect camouflage once the men were flat on the ground.

Once out into populated farmlands, the [main-force] guerrilla [or NVA] columns marched by night, guided by local guerrillas. In this way the [main-force] Viet Cong [or NVA] could normally assemble a complete battalion or more near its target without the enemy suspecting their presence. . . .

The attack itself would began *[sic]* after dark. . . . Again aided by the local guerrillas, the assault force would move up to positions just outside the enemy's defensive perimeter. At zero-hour, a barrage of mortar and rocket fire would pound the target and then guerrillas would storm forward, pressing the fight to close quarters. . . .

. . . But as soon as it was felt that the tactical objectives had been achieved, the order would come to withdraw. The aim was to deny the Americans time to react, and not to be caught by a counter-blow.

Clearing the battlefield was an important part of any operation. The Viet Cong [or NVA] were quite prepared to risk lives to retrieve dead bodies for proper burial. . . . The weapons abandoned by their own dead or wounded and any enemy arms were gathered up, as other soldiers maintained covering fire. As the withdrawal began, a rearguard took up position to deter any pursuit. . . .

The assembly point for the retreating force was usually set about 12 hours march from the scene of the action. . . . Local village guerrillas were always essential for guiding main-force units during a hurried withdrawal in a populated area, because only they knew how to avoid all the booby traps that littered the pathways. They also had the latest information on enemy patrols and could steer the soldiers clear of potential encounters which had to be avoided at all costs.[22]

As there are distinct similarities between the ground assaults of the NVA and Japanese, another trip to Guadalcanal is in order.

Guadalcanal

During the nights of 12 and 13 September 1942, the enemy struck hard at the southern end of the Henderson Field perimeter.

After having prepared (with machineguns, fields of fire, and barbed wire) to defend the ground, Edson's Raiders had to pull back along "Bloody Ridge" three times. "Red Mike's" doubling of the barbed wire after the first night made little difference.[23] The enemy kept coming, and penetrations in the Marines' lines kept occurring:

> . . . [Initially] double apron wire protected the front over the grassy land, while within the jungle there was single strand wire, looped from tree to tree. Fields of fire had been cut here.[24]
>
> — *The Guadalcanal Campaign*
> History Branch, Headquarters Marine Corps

At about 2100 that night [12 September] a Japanese light cruiser and three destroyers entered Sealark Channel to shell the airfield, and at about the same time the enemy ground force probed lightly at the raider-parachute force on the ridge. Fighting was sporadic all along the line, and although one desultory Japanese attack actually made a slight penetration of the Marine line, the enemy made no attempt to consolidate or expand this gain.

Early the next morning (the 13th), Edson launched his counteroffensive, but he found the enemy too strong and well-prepared to be thrown back. In the afternoon the Marine officer withdrew his exhausted men north of the positions they had held the previous night. . . .

In the first hours of darkness . . . Washing-Machine Charley chugged over to drop *his inconsistent scattering of bombs* [italics added], and about 2100 he let go a flare that hung over the field as a registration point for the destroyer task force that now opened up from Sealark Channel.

As if in answer, a flare went up from the troops south of Edson, and without artillery preparation Kawaguchi drove a two-battalion attack against the center and right of the raider-parachute line. Company B's central sector on the high knoll caught most of this first assault and turned it back, but the other attack column found an opening to the west and came through to cut off and envelop Company B's right platoon. While the Japanese drove through this gap

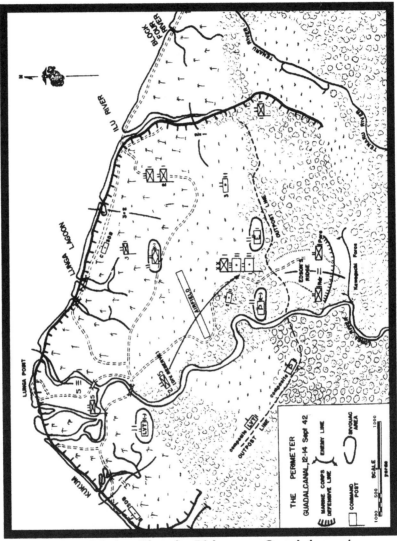

Map 11.1: Bloody Ridge on Guadalcanal

(Source: FMFRP 12-34-I, ▯Pearl Harbor to Guadalcanal,▯ History of the U.S. Marine Corps Operations in World War II, map 18, p. 300)

between Companies A and B, the isolated platoon fought its way back along 250 yards of the ridge to join Company C on the knoll to the north. . . .

Japanese infiltration parties were taking over some of the Company B foxholes, communication lines were cut throughout the area, and the Japanese now began to drum the ridge with heavy mortar fire. Following a violent barrage at 2230, the Japanese attack shifted to the east where it struck the thin flank held by the parachute troops. Screaming in English, "Gas Attack! Gas Attack!", the Japanese came out of the jungle through a smoke screen and drove the parachutists back along the ridge to expose the left flank of Company B.

This left the B Company raiders, now cut to approximately 60 men, exposed on both flanks as well as their front, and Edson called for them to pull back to a last-ditch stand with Company C. Company A would join the force there, and Edson ordered his men to hold at all cost. It was the last dominating terrain feature south of the airfield.[25]

— FMFRP 12-34-I
History of the USMC Operations in WWII

. . . [A]ccording to Lt.Col. [future B.Gen.] Samuel Griffith, the Raider's Executive Officer, the foe actually seized the ridge crest and ". . . would have held it, had not Colonel Edson called for artillery to knock them off. . . . Our 75-mm pack howitzers let go . . . and the shells exploded right under our noses. . . . If that artillery had been a hundred yards short, we'd have been blown to bits with the Japs. . . ."[26]

Before dawn on the 14th, Edson's lines — though now reinforced by the Division reserve battalion — were penetrated by two Japanese companies. One of them made it to Fighter One — the new air strip.

At about 0400, division headquarters began to slip in the companies of the 2d Battalion, 5th Marines to stiffen the line. They helped to fend off two more attacks sent in before dawn, but not all the Japanese were stopped on the ridge. After the decimation of the [Japanese] 5th Company of II/4, the 7th Company continued forward, penetrating a gap in the Marine line and actually reaching the northeast side of the ridge. In this final surge, Major Tamura committed his 6th Company to make a breakthrough. As they passed through the 5th Company, nearly half the fresh unit was hit and the company commander wounded. Nonetheless, the bloodied officer pressed northeast with fifty or sixty men through the Marine position and reached the western fringe of Fighter One about 0530.[27]

... Japanese, evidently from the force that penetrated Edson, wandered into a thin line of Company C, 1st Engineers in the area east of the division CP. . . . [T]he Japanese patrol which struck at 0530 succeeded in taking two left flank machinegun positions. . . . The Japanese heckled the line for the short time remaining until daylight, then retired into the jungle.[28]

— FMFRP 12-34-I
History of USMC Operations in WWII

On the same night at the eastern end of the perimeter, the Kuma Battalion attacked the 3d Battalion, 1st Marine sector. Worried what Japanese infantrymen could do if allowed to get close to Marine lines, Lt. Joe Terzi asked to violate doctrine. His inspiration to establish a "combat listening post" may have saved Henderson Field that night. When Terzi's six Thompson submachinegunners opened up at close range, the Japanese force must have deployed early.[29] With its momentum interrupted, it later fell victim to supporting arms and automatic weapons fire.

For a month and a half, the Marines reinforced their lines with people, barbed wire, and machineguns. When the Japanese struck again near Edson's Ridge near the end of October, they continued to force their way in.

After the struggle for Bloody Ridge, Vandegrift's men had a quiet period which they used to strengthen their defenses around the perimeter. Splinterproof foxholes were dug. Gun emplacements and machinegun posts were strengthened

with log roofs then covered with soil into which fast growing creepers and grasses were placed for natural camouflage. Large areas of grass, beyond the wire perimeter, were
burned to give better fields of fire. On the barbed wire,
Marines hung tin cans and grenades with the pin partly
removed.[30]

By 24 October, 1st Battalion, 7th Marines had twice its normal
number of machineguns and some very proficient machinegunners
(like Sgt. "Manila" John Basilone) guarding its sector.[31] But, that
night, Chesty Puller's boys got more trouble than they had imag-
ined possible — from elements of the Sendai Division.

At about 2130, a Japanese unit clashed briefly with a
46-man outpost Puller had stationed forward of his tactical
wire, but after a short firefight the enemy bypassed the position, and the battlefield was quiet. . . . Puller ordered his
men to hold fire so that Briggs [the platoon sergeant in
charge of the outpost] could infiltrate to safety. . . . Briggs
led his men to the east while the enemy moved closer to
Puller's battalion and began to cut the tactical wire in front
of the 1/7 positions.
While Puller's men strained to hear the approaching
enemy above the sound of drumming rain . . . the Japanese
prepared their routes through the Marine . . . barbed wire
and formed up for their attack. Then at 0030 on 25 October, Nasu's men came out of the jungle screaming their
banzai's, throwing grenades . . . to strike the left center of
1/7's line with an assault in depth on a narrow front. . . .[32]
— FMFRP 12-34-I
History of the USMC Operations in WWII

A wedge was driven into the Marine lines, but eventually
straightened out by repeated counterattacks. . . . He [Puller]
called for reinforcements and the Army's 3d Battalion, 164th
Infantry . . . was ordered forward.[32]
— "First Offensive: Marine Campaign for Guadalcanal"
Marine Corps History and Museums Division

Actually, penetrations occurred at several points along Puller's sector that night;[34] the "wedge" was only the most serious. It was almost 150 yards wide and not removed until the next day,[35] when 37 intruders would be killed inside that particular salient. All told, 250 Japanese — one battalion commander, 24 other officers, and 225 enlisted men (40 of them carrying dynamite and land mines) — would be found dead inside Marine lines.[36] That night a Japanese regimental commander may have also gotten in. He personally led the charge,[37] and it was his elation that caused the Japanese fleet commander to believe that Henderson Field had been captured.

> Having penetrated the American lines, [regimental commander] Furimaya signalled his success to [division commander] Maruyama who misunderstood the message and reported to [army commander] Hyakutake that the airfield had been captured.[38]

Down the line that same night, a group of enemy soldiers crept up on and massacred a three-man outpost from 2d Battalion, 7th Marines.[39] On hearing Japanese chatter where Marines had been, Sgt. Mitchell Paige plastered the area with grenades. When the enemy attacked again the following night, they didn't need the element of surprise to make considerable gains.

> Until midnight [on 25 October] these thrusts were thrown back, but at 0300 an assault swept over [Company F]. . . . In the haze of morning some 150 Japanese, could be observed in F/2/7 foxholes firing American machineguns at adjacent Marine emplacements.[40]
> — FMFRP 12-34-I
> *History of the USMC Operations in WWII*

That 23,000 Marines were now deployed in depth (concentric circles) around Henderson Field played no small part in its defense.[41] Every time a Japanese force penetrated the outer ring, it had to deal with an inner ring and "mop-up" patrols. Still, by whatever means, those Marines and their brethren in arms stopped a very proficient opponent from capturing their three- by nine-mile beachhead. Japanese assault tactics on Guadalcanal bear a striking resemblance to those perfected by German Stormtroopers in WWI,[42] i.e. (1) bangaloring the protective barbed wire during an artillery barrage,[43] and then (2) transiting the breach without shooting any small arms (using bayonets and grenades only so as not to disclose the presence of ground troops).[44] These tactics should have come as no surprise to Marines whose predecessors had helped to blunt the second of the highly successful German Spring offensives of 1918 — in which every enemy infantry squad had been well versed in the technique.[45] By that time, the Germans had been military advisors to the Japanese for over 45 years.[46] Japanese culture comes from the mainland,[47] and this particular attack technique is a perfect example of the common-sense style of warfare first committed to writing by the Chinese in 350 B.C. Despite a lot of lip service to the contrary, Marine squads have to this day been trained almost exclusively in attrition warfare techniques,[48] and, as such, insulated from detailed knowledge of enemy capabilities. Perhaps that's why former Raider Battalion executive officer Samuel Griffith felt it necessary to translate and publish Sun Tzu's *Art of War* in 1963,[49] as U.S. involvement in Vietnam became imminent.

With unlimited resources, American servicemen have been slow to learn that their traditional defensive alignment — even with well positioned barbed wire and interlocking machinegun fire — will not stop this type of attack. While the Japanese did suffer heavy losses during that October attack, their error appears to be not in their squad assault technique, but rather in trying to squeeze too many follow-on forces through each penetration. Forced to pass single file through narrow breaches in the Marines' barbed wire, enemy platoons and companies became vulnerable to final protective fires (preregistered artillery and machineguns on their flanks). If the attacking units had made one breach per squad initially, the battle's outcome might have been different. While transiting protective barbed wire, attrition warfare tenets work better.

The key to stopping ground assaults is interrupting enemy momentum forward of friendly lines. This can best be accomplished by deploying aggressive security patrols, ambushes, and combat listening posts. Those patrolling must have the ability to look for sign (footprints and such), the authority to follow it to its source, and the techniques to attack whoever made it — no matter what their size. Ambushers must rely on claymores and grenades alone so as not to disclose their presence. Those manning combat listening posts must be allowed to shift indirect fire from preregistered targets and blow claymores before withdrawing.

Dealing with Tanks in the Backfield

Occasionally, enemy armor shows up unexpectedly in rear areas. A few tales from the Gulf War and then Vietnam may reveal a better way to prepare for this eventuality.

(Source: FM 17-1 (1966), p. 179)

The Gulf War

What first comes to mind is killing tanks from the air. In Kuwait, all airstrikes were closely controlled by higher headquarters. Because of the perceived electronic warfare threat (jamming and countermeasures), U.S. forces had to use sophisticated radio equipment and rotating transmission codes. One U.S. Army forward air controller later admitted that the rotation of codes so complicated the airstrikes that it had to be discontinued early in the war.[50]

The Marines overcontrolled their close air support in the Gulf as well. While any good E-4 can be trained to run a modern airstrike (complete with suppression-of-enemy-air-defenses artillery mission), Marine snipers hiding in Khafji were not authorized to do so. Had they been, they might have single-handedly stopped the Iraqi tanks well short of the city.[51] On an active battlefield (one on which hundreds of contacts with the enemy occur simultaneously), how counterproductive could it be to let squad leaders control their own airstrikes over uncovered, VHF company nets? Just the plethora of transmissions would be enough to confuse most eavesdroppers.

Vietnam and Earlier Asian Conflicts

The NVA didn't need tanks to defeat the most powerful nation on earth in Vietnam. They only resorted to armor a few times. Once was at the Lang Vei Special Forces Camp in 1968. While the enemy only fielded lightly armored PT-76 amphibious tanks, the Green Berets had to rely on the replacement to the 3.5-inch rocket launcher, the M72 LAAW. Point blank fire could do nothing more than break the track on one NVA tank.[52]

During this period in history, one could spot a Marine tanker by the beads of sweat on his forehead. Except for a light-section leader by the name of Gy.Sgt. Silva (who would charge across the rice paddies as the spirit moved him), most Marine tankers ran into trouble before getting close to any major ground action.[53] Their nemesis was probably a spider hole occupant with an antitank mine on a string. Japanese antitank troops used a similar procedure throughout WWII.[54] Tanks traveling behind infantry were also vulnerable to RPG rockets from spider holes.

It would appear that small, covert outposts are the key to killing unexpected enemy armor. They can do so without being noticed by (1) acting as spotters for supporting arms, or (2) operating from spider holes with antitank mines or rockets. U.S. units could enhance their defensive posture by tasking a few of their two-man observation posts with secondary anti-armor-protection missions.

12 Doing More with Less in Peacetime

- *Is there any excuse for not bettering squad tactics?*
- *How can more training be done without more time?*

(Source: FM 22-100 (1983), p. 255)

What's over the Horizon Tactically

Modern war is about the dispersion of troops and the decentralization of control over them. Enemy weapon systems have become so lethal that forward elements cannot safely operate at larger than squad size for long. A single fuel air explosive can take out an entire rifle company. Unfortunately, U.S. infantry squads lack the tactical expertise to maneuver semi-independently against superior numbers. Military leaders genuinely interested in minimizing casualties must find some way to improve small-unit tactics. As with any change, they must first counter a variety of excuses.

A Lack of Funding

There's never "enough money" to train. It's true that military spending cuts occur during peacetime. The various branches of the service are not given lump sums to spend any way they want. Their requirements have to be budgeted, and then the Department of Defense initiatives with the most political support generally get funded. This process — by its very nature — creates chronic fiscal shortfalls. For example, personnel and training man-days come out of the same pot of money. Because adjusting end strength (manning levels) takes time, formal schooling suffers. But training can be accomplished elsewhere. In fact, at the unit level, the shortage of funding presents little problem. Preparing for common-sense warfare takes no money.

Modern warfighters rely more on movement than on shooting skills. They don't need to "go to the field" or "live fire their small-arms" to train on tactics; they can do that with rubber rifles in the woods behind their barracks. They are more interested in generating surprise than in hitting distant targets. Because surprise is the product of stealth, speed, and deception, it can be measured by (1) how close an attacker can get undetected, (2) how fast he can move, and (3) how unpredictable he can become. Because an attacker's ability to avoid detection will be inversely proportional to his losses, degree of surprise can also be measured by simulated casualty totals. The U.S. military has MILES gear — laser emission devices that affix to weapons and laser impact alarms that attach to warbelts and helmets. Because this gear is in short supply and temperamental, units often prefer casualty assessment alternatives. Counting flour grenades that land within 10 feet of oneself and three-second sight pictures of upright opponents works nicely. Further, sand table demonstrations and group discussions of progressive-book chapters cost nothing.

No Time

Then, there's always a "shortage of training time." What those who resort to this excuse are really saying is that they don't have the time to save lives. It's true that today's peacetime military is the most heavily committed in history. And the flow of headquarters red tape has grown to monumental proportions. Yet again, what unit leaders generally perceive as a time shortage presents little problem.

Only battalion and company staffs stay busy all the time — doing mostly administrative housekeeping. Even on busy days, infantry squads experience delays between scheduled events. During major exercises, they spend long periods doing nothing. Battledrills or situational stations only take 20 minutes to perform. Strung together, they could constitute a significant training evolution.

The Shortage of Trained Instructors

Finally, there's never "enough school-trained instructors." Most formal schools are forced to limit their curriculum to what's in the manuals. The battlefield has changed a lot since those manuals were written. They contain mostly technique (as opposed to doctrine) anyway — ways of solving certain sets of circumstances. Unfortunately, the manuals don't specify those circumstances in detail. A shortage of book-trained people doesn't constitute much of a handicap.

As junior enlisted personnel must compete for promotion from the standpoint of relative book knowledge, a few make the mistake of using tactical drills to build discipline in peacetime and book solutions to solve any situation in war. The U.S. small-unit tactics manual procedures are no longer useful as techniques — they lack the surprise to generate minimal casualties. They are still useful, however, as guidelines — as frameworks within which to develop viable tactical methods. And those who would totally discount what they contain are throwing away 200 years of institutional knowledge. The vast majority of NCO's keep book learning in proper perspective. They are by nature team-oriented, inquisitive, and talkative people. In their search for better ways to do things, they are not above asking subordinates for the answer. Every NCO is a potential instructor.

Let Someone Else Make It Happen

Now that U.S. commanders realize that a properly trained buddy team or squad can often accomplish what used to take a company or battalion, they have an obligation to do something about it. After all, where fewer personnel are involved, fewer have to go into harm's way. The problem will be what to do. The commanders need a way — without many assets — to improve small-unit tactical techniques while instilling initiative and decision-making skills at the lowest echelons of their units. They will need a different training method and someone else to make it happen. This method need not be revolutionary, but it must harness the collective common sense of those whose job it is to perform small-unit tactics — the NCO's. Only a well seasoned SNCO can bring NCO's together to produce what's required.

> Never tell people how to do things. Tell them what to do and they will surprise you with their ingenuity.[1]
> — Patton

13 An Interim Solution for Units

● *How can the NCO learn tactical decision making?*

● *What role must the leader/instructor play?*

(Source: Corel Gallery, Clickart, Weapons, 45A123)

An Overview of the Problem

Warfare has become much more complicated since 1975. In WWI, WWII, Korea, and Vietnam, U.S. infantrymen faced artillery shells, machinegun bullets, and trip flares. Now they face smart bombs, grenade throwing machineguns, and thermal imaging. Any one of these modern marvels of mayhem can seal the fate of an entire attack force. But, to counter almost any advance in enemy weapons technology, an infantry unit has only to adequately subdivide and spread out its subunits. Nothing bigger than a squad can sneak up on a prepared enemy position anyway. That makes the squad the maneuver element of the future and the NCO its tactical decision maker. The NCO who is only allowed to follow orders and shoot his weapons will not be ready for that role. But there is a way to prepare him. It's not by removing him from his understrength unit to attend a formal school; it's by requiring him to help run a "supplementary" training schedule — one that can be accomplished during delays in his unit's already full agenda. If every NCO were required to design, conduct, and refine a key component to a well-thought-out company training evolution, he would be forced to learn from the collective common sense of seniors, peers, and subordinates alike.

World-class squads do most of their tactical decision making before the battle starts. That's the way they develop momentum. Below is outlined an innovative way with which infantry companies can acquire maneuver warfare capabilities at the squad level and below.

A New Style of Training Will Be Required

To become maneuver warfare capable, infantry companies must learn to function under decentralized control — i.e., to operate as 12 semi-independent squads. In combat, units squad-sized or smaller can capture momentum the way football teams do — by operating off prerehearsed plays. Before each battle, the squad must develop and practice several numbered techniques for each expected category of combat situation. When the enemy shows up, the squad leader and fire team leaders can then quickly confer by hand-and-arm signals on which play to use. As in football, circumstances will seldom allow any one technique to be run exactly as rehearsed. Squad members must have the authority to improvise as necessary. What results is a series of rapid solutions to unique situations. With enough practice, squads can come close to transcending technique. Unpredictability and momentum give fire teams, buddy teams, and individuals a better chance to prevail as well. As in football, they too must practice several "moves" for each expected encounter.

In common-sense warfare, control is attained through training and then apprising superiors of actions taken. Time-consuming orders and leadership are only necessary in attrition war.

Because the new training method must instill initiative and tactical-decision-making ability at the lowest echelons, it must mirror the tactics — recon pull instead of command push. Elements that operate semi-independently no longer require identical methods. Only through experimentation and innovation can the lower echelons of a tall organization stay up with an ever-changing threat.

The daily training regimen for a rifle squad should resemble that of a football team too — squad, fire team, buddy team, and individual drills followed by force-on-force scrimmaging. Because initiative and tactical decision making cannot be taught per se, the officers would be well advised to remember how they were trained at Officer Candidate School. They must control this training indirectly. They can do so by (1) choosing situations to be solved (specifying terrain, aggressor positions, and casualty assessment methods), (2) providing historical examples of possible solutions, (3) not requiring strict reenactment of book procedures, and (4) only demanding improvement on surprise (speed, stealth, or deception) or casualties suffered. The company commander will have to settle for issuing a "mission type" training order to his gunnery sergeant. Platoon commanders will have to work through their platoon sergeants. Platoon sergeants, squad leaders, and fire team leaders will have to let subordinates help to design their own methods.

> The gunnery sergeant . . . is the principal enlisted assistant to the company commander in supervising the training of the company.[1]
> — FMFM 6-4
> *Marine Rifle Company / Platoon*

The Planning Phase

As a group, the officers give the company gunnery sergeant a short list of squad situations to be solved. Best are those involving large numbers of enemy, because they need total surprise to succeed (e.g., security patrolling against a well hidden enemy battalion). Others might address counterambushing, ambushing, chance contact, defense, day attack, night attack, short-range infiltration attack, urban attack, or urban defense.

In turn, the gunnery sergeant convenes a conference of all the NCO's in the company. Acting only as facilitator, he helps the group to arrive at a list of composite skills for each situation — what squads, fire teams, buddy teams, and individuals must be able to do to accomplish the officers' goals. Emphasized will be those aspects of the standard "basics" that don't telegraph intentions — more crawling, less small-arms shooting, and less ostentatious signaling. Instruction on some new fundamentals will be required: (1) seeing, (2) not being seen, (3) hearing, (4) not being heard, (5) passive-defense measures (like taking cover), and (6) tactical decision making.

A training schedule is now developed with the proper progression of composite skills (individual skills first). Weapons training can have one of two formats: (1) explain, demonstrate, imitate, practice, test; or (2) create a situation for students to solve (more retention and applicability to enemy weapons). Established tactical skills will be taught through battledrills: (1) attention gainer, (2) lecture, (3) demonstration, (4) practical application, and (5) practical application testing. New tactical skills will be investigated through "situational stations" in which students arrive at collective answers. Tactical methods must be retaught in several different formats — e.g. historical example, blackboard sketch, sand table model, outdoor demonstration, and then outdoor practice — to reach every learning style.

Next, an NCO is assigned to each period of instruction. Leaders of the next-higher echelon must do the teaching so as not to undermine subunit leader authority (e.g. fire team leaders teach buddy teams and individuals). Instructors with pronounced attrition warfare attitudes — like those who think that war is about killing or that privates are stupid — are given situational stations to run. Tactics instructors are told to use *The Last Hundred Yards* from Posterity Press as their source document. (Added to the "Commandant's Current Issues Reading List" by ALMAR 152/98, this book contains the product of 10 years of research involving 1200 Marine NCO's — doctrinally correct, fully staffed and tested common-sense techniques.)

Learning to move will be emphasized over learning to shoot, so the instruction can take place anywhere with makeshift training aids (no live fire required).

The Execution Phase

"Technique Training" can be accomplished sequentially or in round-robin format (as time permits). Most training will be done in 20-minute blocks with 12-man groups. To do a whole unit, an instructor just asks his peers to help. To train 36 Marines, competition between three of the smaller groups would work. Tactical techniques are practiced twice (the second time in different terrain) to demonstrate that they can't be run again precisely as rehearsed. Success is measured by better speed or stealth (or fewer casualties) on successive tries. Freely admitting mistakes is encouraged; instructors view a student's doing poorly as possibly providing tactical insight into an unresolved problem.

Next, comes the "Tactical Demonstration." Officers arrange all training support to recreate the exact situations they had in mind. The squads take turns solving those situations under simulated fire (as produced by artillery and machinegun simulators) and casualty assessment procedures. When the demonstrations have concluded, the officers tell the NCO's whether their expectations have been met.

Then there's "Free Play" — a force-on-force exercise in which the side accomplishing its mission with the least casualties wins. Sides are generally required to reverse their shirts and man static positions a few hundred yards apart with one-third their strength. Those comprised of infantrymen must attack each other's defensive position twice. Those comprised of noninfantrymen must make chance contact, ambush, or counterambush each other's patrols twice. While losses can be assessed with MILES gear, having individuals record flour-grenade impacts within 10 feet of themselves or three-second sight pictures of upright opponents works nicely. After 10 minutes and promising not to divulge enemy locations, casualties may reenter the exercise as replacements. Switching uniforms, using a vehicle, or touching an opposition player earns 10 demerits. Secretly seizing the other side's flag nets 30 bonus points. A minimum of four umpires are required — one with each static position and maneuver element. At a pre-established time, those empires (1) separate the sides, (2) account for all personnel, (3) add up losses, demerits, and bonus points, and then (4) designate a winner.

Last comes the "Lessons-Learned Field Day." The gunnery sergeant assembles the whole company and asks for volunteers to demonstrate better ways of doing things. By gauging each idea's worth through a show of hands, he can tell whether the privates' expectations have been met.

The Supervision Phase

Supervision happens concurrently throughout the training cycle. Better speed/stealth/deception and fewer casualties on successive tries guarantees better tactics. Collective common sense of enlisted men (peer pressure) ensures dynamic parity between companies. At the Tactical Demonstration, the officers tell NCO's whether their expectations have been met. At the Lessons-Learned Field Day, privates get the chance (through a show of hands) to identify as-yet-unresolved problems and alternative solutions. To initiate a new training cycle, the officers revise their list of situations, and the NCO's modify their list of prerequisite skills. If the company gunnery sergeant doesn't produce fewer casualties during the Tactical Demonstrations than on previous occasions, he may have to relinquish the role of company trainer to one of his staff sergeants.

The Incredible End Result

By learning this way during delays in the normal training schedule, units can (1) improve morale/cohesion, (2) reduce disciplinary problems, (3) modernize individual through squad tactics, (4) lighten their logistical burden, (5) show leaders when and where to fight, and (6) experience fewer casualties — friendly, enemy, and civilian.

When an entire day can be devoted to this type of training, battledrills or situational stations take up the morning, squad rehearsals and force-on-force scrimmaging the afternoon.

This alternative way of learning works. Of hundreds of Marines polled after exposure to "bottom-up" training, 98% preferred it to the standard "top-down" variety. As of May 1999, two thirds of all active-duty Marine infantry battalions had received instruction on its use, and several had put it into practice.[2]

14 The Real Need: Military Reform

- *Why cannot the system keep up with the threat?*
- *Could bottom-up training solve the problem?*

(Source: FM 22-100 (1983), p. 103)

Admitting Past Mistakes

While Americans may view integrity as their most valued asset, many have chosen to ignore ongoing discrepancies between predeployment claims and battlefield performance. Where hands-on knowledge has difficulty traveling up the chain of command, could not a military organization lose sight of what it takes to succeed at the lowest echelon? The U.S. Armed Forces may be the best in the world overall, but not in the area of individual or small-unit tactics.

Since 1941 . . . our forces were not as well trained as those

of the enemy. . . . After the buildup of forces, when we went on the offensive, we did not defeat the enemy tactically. We overpowered and overwhelmed our enemies with equipment and fire power.[1]
　　　　　— Lt.Gen. Arthur S. Collins, Jr., U.S. Army (Ret.)

The American public may have rallied to save its fighting men from an equipment shortage during WWII, but it has never tried to save them from overcentralized control.

The decentralization of tactical control forced on land forces has been one of the most significant features of modern war. In the confused and often chaotic environment of today, only the smallest groups are likely to keep together, particularly during critical moments.[2]

Although combat experience should indicate otherwise, the rifle squad currently occupies a relatively minor place in . . . [U.S.] tactical thought. Squad level training and doctrine seem to suggest that the squad has little independent tactical value. The squad has been relegated to the role of subunit whose movements are closely controlled by the platoon commander. Considered in terms of maneuver [common-sense] warfare, this attitude is disastrous . . . (maneuver warfare demands that the squad assume a primary tactical role).[3]
　　　　　— Bill Lind
　　　　　　personal advisor to 29th Marine commandant

Right after WWII, U.S. citizens may have saved countless thousands of Europeans with the Marshall Plan. But since then, they have abused enemy noncombatants and killed their friends with too much ordnance instead of properly trained troops.

[Future Lt.Gen.] Puller often heard these officers [his instructors] admit that they did not know the answers he was constantly seeking. In truth, it seemed that little had been written about his favorite topic — limited, small-scale combat.[4]

With the Berlin Airlift, Americans may have circumvented a blockade to preserve freedom, but they have still to give U.S. soldiers enough leeway to save their own lives.

The U.S. military may have countered aggression in Korea, but it also killed two million civilians with a 600,000-ton bombing campaign,[5] which had no strategic effect on the enemy's resupply effort.[6] This might have qualified as an unfortunate mistake, if something similar hadn't been well documented a few years before. In December 1945, the *U.S. Strategic Bombing Survey* reported that German industrial production had actually increased during the Allied bombing campaign.[7] Upwards of three million noncombatants died that time.[8]

> None of the bombing did any good. German industry went underground and spread out.[9]
> — member of Strategic Bombing Survey Team
> *Last Days of World War II* on History Channel

U.S. forces may have halted Communism's domino effect in Vietnam, but outmoded infantry tactics cost the lives of 56,000 Americans and a million of the very people they were trying to rescue.[10] After two tours, America's most highly decorated veteran pointed out that U.S. knowledge on small-unit tactics had not been significantly enhanced by the longest war in U.S. history:

> . . . [S]ince the tragic, inevitable fall of Saigon, there has been no major, honest post mortem of the war. There have been critiques dealing with the big picture . . . but none has addressed the lessons learned the hard way, at the fighting level, where people died and the war was in fact, lost.[11]
> — Col. David H. Hackworth U.S. Army (Ret.)

Americans may have shortstopped evil by bankrupting their Cold War arms race opponent, but they have yet to demand proficiency in the more moral of the two well established styles of war. To harness the common sense of those who do the fighting, an army must decentralize control. One wonders how the U.S. military would fare on a simple control assessment questionnaire.

Centralized Control	**Decentralized Control**
_ Fitness Report Establishes Who Is Easiest to Lead	_ Fit. Rep. Shows Who's Tactically Proficient
_ Job Assignments Based on Equitable Rotation	_ Job Assignments Based on Expertise
_ Field Manuals Promoted As Pure Doctrine	_ FM's Admit to Being Mostly Technique
_ Schools Required to Use Same Essential Learning Objectives	_ Instructors Allowed to Add Other ELO's
_ Headquarters' Initiatives Drive Operational Tempo	_ Units Decide How to Best Use Their Time
_ Hdqts. Dictates Individual and Small-Unit Training Standards	_ Units Ascertain Own Training Needs
_ Units Are Rank Top-Heavy or Cadred	_ Units Have Enough of the Junior Ranks
_ Higher Ranks Perform Functions Lower Ranks Should	_ Authority Delegated As Much As Possible
_ Technological Advances Appear to Lessen Need for Basic Skills	_ Basic Skills Viewed As Irreplaceable
_ More Knowledge on Everything Associated with Higher Rank	_ Lower Ranks Seen As Basics Experts

Table 14.1: Control Assessment Questionnaire

(Source: FM 22-100 (1983), p. 266)

Overwhelming Force Is Not the Answer

Americans have grown suspicious of the consumerism, rugged individualism, and superiority that have come to dominate their culture. They worry that U.S. society has become too violent. While they work to curtail that violence in their streets, many still regard aerial bombardment as a valuable instrument of foreign policy.

First, we are taught that the world is a dangerous place and that human beings are intrinsically violent. This is particularly true of our enemies who are the *most* violent and beyond redemption or change. Faced with these cold

103

facts, we learn our second lesson: the only way to deal with violence is to accommodate it, avoid it, or use violence ourselves. . . .

The great illusion of violence is that it will solve our problems decisively. Unfortunately, conflicts often do not end when violence is used; they generally continue to smolder or escalate.

Violence 101's ultimate lesson is that violence feeds on itself and cannot be extinguished; there is always residual resentment and injustice. . . .

The world can be dangerous. . . . But are we condemned to an endless cycle of retaliation and domination? The traditional responses to violence often make matters worse because they fail to address root causes and they lose sight of the integrity of those in conflict. . . .

Violence separates us from others. It defiles the human person and desecrates the image of God. It is a process of economic, racial, social or cultural domination. . . . Transforming these patterns of destructiveness is a sacred journey from fear to freedom, from despair to hope. . . .[12]

Bombs will never be smart enough to distinguish between underground command posts and air raid shelters, biological warfare sites and vaccine producing facilities, or government office spaces and foreign embassy compounds. Every time an errant bomb kills someone's mother, the U.S. creates another potential terrorist. Machines can't make last-second moral decisions, only properly trained ground troops (or policemen) can do that — personnel who know how to win without a lot of firepower. Using more or bigger ordnance seldom achieves timely closure. Pentagon procurers have been slow to admit that human beings can outsmart machines.

The Time for Change is Now

U.S. voters still control the world's best chance for peace. As such, they have a sacred responsibility to do the right thing — to push for military reform. After affirming every man's right to life, liberty, and the pursuit of happiness, the *Declaration of Indepen-*

dence goes on to say, "That to secure these rights, Governments are instituted among Men, deriving their just powers from the consent of the governed. That whenever any Form of Government becomes destructive of these ends, it is the Right of the People to alter . . . it."[13]

It's clear that small-unit infantry knowledge doesn't build upon itself like other types of knowledge. The nations that pioneered common-sense warfare have at times been tempted (mostly by technology) to discount its precepts. For example, the Russians became roadbound in Afghanistan and Chechnya. Tactical evolution appears to depend, not so much on new knowledge per se, but on how it is generated within the military organization. The squad techniques adopted by the Germans late in 1917 hadn't just been acquired from the Japanese or the Boers. Before sharing the stormtrooper method for breaching enemy lines with General Ludendorff, Capt. Rohr may have just learned it from his NCO's. The real catalyst for this growth was the decentralized control over training that existed in the German Army at that time. In other words, the knowledge was being generated from the bottom up instead of from the top down. German NCO's were considered to be tactical decision makers, and company commanders could train anyway they wanted. German Army Headquarters did, of course, have the foresight to widely disseminate what had been learned

(Source: FMFM 2-1 (1967), p. 129)

105

in this manner — namely, new offensive and defensive squad tactics and how to train for them. With the squad techniques in *The Last Hundred Yards* and the training methodology in this book, U.S. rifle companies will have the same opportunity.

Military manuals and training standards can't adequately reflect the corporate knowledge of a great military organization anyway. Even if they could, the long chain of command creates too much opportunity for some middle manager to misrepresent those standards. Until U.S. infantry manuals are perceived as broad guidelines, training standards as partial minimums, self criticism as the way to improve, experimentation and free play as the best learning method, U.S. small-unit tactics will lag behind those of Eastern nations. Until momentum and unpredictability are made available to small-unit and individual soldier alike, close contact with the enemy will continue to cost too much. The glorification of rank does little to achieve this end.

> Prejudice against innovation is a typical characteristic of an Officer Corps which has grown up in a well-tried and proven system.[14]
> — Field Marshal Erwin Rommel

15 Decentralizing Control Works

- *Can defense establishments decentralize control?*
- *What examples are there in the Western World?*

(Source: FM 7-93 (1987), cover)

A Societal Oversight Badly in Need of Fixing

Just outlined has been the solution to a major failure of U.S. intentions — the wholesale sacrifice of American youth to outmoded small-unit infantry tactics. Societies and organizations suffer from bad habits just as people do. Some problems progressively diminish — like the shifting from apartheid to a more representative form of government in South Africa; or moving from slavery, to integration, and finally into equal opportunity in this country. But other societal ills become more pronounced over time — like the breaking down of the all-important family unit.

As with personal sin, societal indiscretions are difficult to identify. Many Americans agree that genocide is evil, but discarding 1.4
million innocents a year doesn't seem to bother them. Occasionally,
shifts in morality become legalized in the name of progress — e.g.
the killing of Jews in WWII Germany. For almost 200 years, the
U.S. legal system told its citizens that abortion was wrong; then, in
1962, it made a single exception. Now the majority of Americans
apparently believe that a young mother can do herself no harm by
discarding an integral part of her body and soul — her joint venture
with God. Saving the lives of American soldiers might be the first
step back along the road to Constitutional values. Military reform
could be the intermediate stop on the way to lasting peace.

> The only thing necessary for evil to triumph is for good men
> to do nothing.[1]
> — Edmund Burke
> British political figure from the 18th century

Appearances Can Be Deceiving in War Too

Military organizations require discipline. Respect for rank helps
to produce coordination. Rules and regulations help to establish
acceptable norms. What military organizations sometimes fail to
realize is that too much control can undermine that discipline. Is it
not self control that produces more moral or effective behavior in
other aspects of life? What each soldier does when his leader is not
around is often what counts most. Certainly, every soldier must be
taught the difference between right and wrong. But the difference
between truth and fiction is just as important. Instead of being
encouraged to "rat" on their friends, perhaps Oriental soldiers are
taught to tell the truth. If every unit member had integrity and
some influence on command decisions, wouldn't those decisions tend
to be more moral and effective? Was My Lai sparked by inherently
evil soldiers, or misplaced unit priorities? The enlisted members of
one Marine company wouldn't burn a VC hut.[2]

As the foe seldom cooperates, control gets decentralized in combat anyway. Why doesn't the U.S. military practice looser control
in peacetime? Without errors, there can be no learning.

Illusion — Centralized control produces more moral and
effective infantrymen, plus fewer casualties.

Problem — In war, the morality of an act can be measured
by how many people (of any type) it spares.

Problem — In war, the effectiveness of an act has little
to do with how many enemy soldiers it hurts.

Problem — In war, a soldier's life often depends on his
freedom to react to unforeseen circumstances.

Problem — In war, timely decisions are made by echelons
directly in contact with an unpredictable foe.

Problem — In war, when control is centralized, small
units and individuals don't get the leeway to
properly solve or exploit a changing situation.

Problem — In peace, when control is centralized,
small-unit leaders and individuals get little
chance to practice tactical decision making.

Reality — Decentralized control produces infantrymen
with more self control, initiative, and
survivability in war.

Table 15.1: The Battlefield Casualty Paradox

Precedents for Organizational Reform

To preserve limited resources, many Eastern European and
Asian armies long ago figured out how to decentralize control.
Throughout the 20th century, they have displayed the ability to

subdivide into semi-independent yet mutually supporting elements. As their opponents' weapon systems have grown larger, those elements have grown smaller.

> Whether in guerrilla ... or limited regular warfare, waged artfully, it [armed struggle] is fully capable of ... getting the better of a modern army like the U.S. Army. ... This is a development of the ... military art, the main content of which is to rely chiefly on [the] man, on his patriotism and ... spirit, to bring into full play all weapons and techniques available to defeat an enemy with up-to-date weapons and equipment.3
> — General Vo Nguyen Giap
> *The Military Art of Peoples War*

> I'm afraid we haven't recognized the most important lesson from Korea. The Communists have developed a totally new kind of warfare. ... This is a total warfare, yet small in scope, and it's designed to neutralize our big ... weapons. Look at Vietnam. The French outnumbered the Communists two to one, yet they [the French] were massacred.4
> — Chesty Puller

> My prayer now is that our leaders, knowing that we have no war machine, will evacuate Korea completely, have a thorough house cleaning, and then rebuild a real war machine before becoming involved in another war. May God give us wisdom and common sense!5
> — Chesty Puller
> when sent home from Korea and retired

By decentralizing control, Eastern armies have effectively harnessed the common sense of their enlisted members — the expertise in fundamentals that always resides at the lower echelons of any organization. They have also eliminated the need to appease superiors — to keep quiet about mistakes that might cost someone his job. How those non-Western armies managed to achieve similar organizational goals with looser control parameters is still a matter of conjecture. They have done at least three things differently: (1) kept rank in better perspective, (2) relied more on consensus opinions, and (3) participated in more public self-criticism sessions. To them, rank does not mean knowing more about every subordinate's job than he does himself. To them, polling subordinates on what do next does not constitute poor leadership. And to them, asking subordinates what went wrong doesn't jeopardize authority. Perhaps they have come to the realization that strict loyalty to immediate superiors produces what amounts to a "code of silence." What a future U.S. Marine Raider commander learned while observing Mao Tse-tung's 8th Route Army in China during the late thirties helped to sway the battle for Guadalcanal. What the NVA did after every engagement in Vietnam helped to win the war:

> Colonel Carlson had some very specific ideas about training his men, and one was to indoctrinate them with the same sort of democratic spirit as that practiced in the 8th Route Army. There was very little distinction between officers and men, and the slogan of the 2nd Marine Raider Battalion was "gung ho," or "work together," a slogan borrowed directly from the Chinese communists. In fact, later, when the methods of operation of the battalion became known to the public, this slogan and Carlson's techniques aroused a good deal of criticism in Congress and elsewhere, and some questioned Carlson's loyalties because he used techniques derived from the Chinese communists.[6]

> ... In *Kiem thao* sessions, the [North Vietnamese] soldiers offered judgments of their comrades and listened to evaluations of their own performances. The meetings sometimes featured discussions of tactics from the unit's recent engagements or suggestions . . . sent from the army command.
> *Kiem thao* sessions could become extremely heated and emotional. For some soldiers the sessions were especially traumatic, as they heard their weaknesses and failings denounced publicly and then had to respond to those charges.[7]

Of the Western armies, only the Germans have been able to

follow suit. By the end of 1917, they had put their NCO's in charge of small units spearheading ground attacks,[8] and autonomous forts comprising elastic defenses.[9]

> The same decentralization of authority that had permitted the development of stormtroop tactics in the first place also played an important role in its dissemination. . . . The freedom . . . resulted in the troops receiving training with a wide variety of emphases.[10]

> While the British [in WWI] were successful in copying the outward appearance of the German defensive system, they were unable to adopt its substance. The key to the German elastic defense was its reliance upon the initiative and good judgment of the man on the spot, whether he were a sergeant in command of a squad or a captain. . . . [S]uch reliance on junior commanders was an anathema to a system of command that valued, above all else, adherence to established procedure.[11]

> The French, in particular, had a number of bright young officers who proposed tactical reforms similar to those being adopted by the Germans. While these proposals were warmly received by high-ranking officers, they got lost in the bureaucracy and had little effect on the way the French infantry actually fought. . . .
> Neither the French NCO's nor those company officers who had been commissioned after long service as NCO's were considered capable of the kind of independent action, that . . . was universally expected of the German NCO's.[12]

Decentralization alone, however, cannot explain the entire phenomenon of German successes with tactical innovation. The Italian Army of World War I, being like the German Army, a relatively recent amalgamation of the armies of subnational states, was also quite decentralized. While decentralization permitted the Italians to develop the *Arditi* units to such a high degree, it did not cause ordinary infantry units to change the way that they fought. The Italians thus had the means of developing new infantry tactics, but not of disseminating them.[13]

But there's another "defense establishment" in the Western World that has decentralized control — the Roman Catholic Church. After all, its mission is not unlike that of a military organization. While armed forces protect their homelands from aggression, church organizations protect society from the counterspirit. The evil one and his legions of fallen angels are every bit as dangerous as any aggressor army, because they have the power to influence men's minds while remaining invisible themselves. Like a church, every military unit needs a chain of command to keep its members from overstepping their bounds. But, also like a church, every military unit must allow its members enough initiative to react to the situations at hand.

To more effectively perform its mission, the Roman Catholic Church officially decentralized control in 1962. As a result of the Second Vatican Council, responsibility for solving societal problems shifted over to the nonclerical (or lay) majority. While Catholics constitute the world's largest denomination (almost 1 billion at last count),[14] their method of helping their neighbors was to be as simple as it was nonintrusive. Each was to spread the word of Christ through setting a good example. As bureaucracies seldom relinquish control, this event quite literally qualifies as a miracle.

The redemptive work of Jesus extends to every aspect of life in the world. There is no other solution to the problems of the world.[15]
— "The Dogmatic Constitution of the Church"
Second Vatican Council

The Laity must take on the renewal of the temporal order as their own special obligation. Led by the insight of the gospel, and the mind of the Church [of which Jesus is the head], and motivated by Christian love, let them act directly and definitively in the temporal sphere [world].[16]
— "Decree of the Apostolate of the Laity"
Second Vatican Council

Perhaps it's time for another Western defense establishment with Christian ideals to follow suit. Only then will the U.S. military be able to fully practice what amounts to a more moral and effective way of performing its mission. And only then will it be able to minimize its losses. To evolve into a world-class fighting force, it must come to respect the individual soldier and noncombatant alike. "Taking care" of one's troops means more than just feeding, clothing, and paying them — it means helping them to achieve their full potential as human beings. America has always intended to safeguard its citizens, but those intentions haven't always been realized. If they had, U.S. prisons wouldn't be full of minorities, and legalized abortion wouldn't have claimed 37 million American children.[17]

Until Americans as a people acknowledge the truth about morality and effectiveness in war, they dishonor all who have died to keep them free. Yes, there will be growth pains. Those who place power and money above all else may suffer a little discomfort. Military leaders may have to admit that their subordinates are collectively smarter than they are. Military ordnance salesmen may have to settle for smaller profit margins. Defense industry jobs may be lost, and maybe even a few votes. But, in the eyes of the global community, a great nation's moral integrity will again light the road to world peace.

> The whole of man's history has been the story of dour combat with the powers of evil, stretching, so our Lord tells us, from the very dawn of history until the last day. Finding himself in the midst of the battlefield man has to struggle to do what is right, and it is at great cost to himself, and aided by God's grace, that he succeeds in achieving his own inner integrity (GS 37 § 2).[18]

Notes

SOURCE NOTES

Reprinted with permission of the Greenwood Publishing Group Inc., Westport, CT, from *STORMTROOP TACTICS — INNOVATION IN THE GERMAN ARMY 1914-1918,* by Bruce I. Gudmundsson. Copyright © 1989 by Bruce I. Gudmundsson. All rights reserved.

Reprinted with permission of the National Secretariat of the Cursillo Movement, P.O. Box 210226 Dallas, TX 75211, from *THE THREE DAYS (LAITY).* Copyright © 1982 by the National Secretariat of the Cursillo Movement. All rights reserved.

Reprinted with permission of Brandt & Brandt Literary Agents, New York, NY, from *A TIME FOR TRUMPETS,* by Charles B. McDonald. Copyright © 1985 by Charles B. McDonald. All rights reserved.

Reprinted with permission of Boston Publishing Co., Inc., 85 Wells Ave., Suite 200, Newton, MA 02159, from *VIETNAM EXPERIENCE: A CONTAGION OF WAR,* by Terrence Maitland and Peter McInerny. Copyright © 1983 by Boston Publishing Co. All rights reserved.

Reprinted with permission of Houghton Mifflin Co., from *WAR AS I KNEW IT,* by Gen. George S. Patton. Copyright © 1947 by Beatrice Patton Walters, Ruth Patton Totten and George Smith Totten. Copyright © renewed 1975 by Maj.Gen. George Patton, Ruth Patton Totten, John K. Waters Jr., and George P. Waters. All rights reserved.

Reprinted with permission of Time-Life Books, from *WORLD WAR II: BOMBERS OVER JAPAN,* by Keith Wheeler and the editors of Time-Life Books. Copyright © 1982 by Time-Life Books, Inc. All rights reserved.

Reprinted with permission of Time-Life Books, from *WORLD WAR II: THE BATTLE OF THE BULGE,* by William K. Goolirck and Ogden Tanner and the editors of Time-Life Books. Copyright © 1979 by Time-Life Books, Inc. All rights reserved.

Reprinted with permission of Time-Life Books, from *WORLD WAR II: THE HOME FRONT U.S.A.,* by Ronald H. Bailey and the editors of Time-Life Books. Copyright © 1977 by Time-Life Books, Inc. All rights reserved.

Reprinted with permission of Random House, Inc., from *WW II: THE ENCYCLOPEDIA OF THE WAR YEARS 1941-1945,* by Norman Polmar and Thomas B. Allen. Copyright © 1996 by Norman Polmar and Thomas B. Allen. All rights reserved.

ENDNOTES

Preface

1. *True Stories of World War II,* ed. Nancy J. Sparks (Pleasantville, NY: Readers Digest Assoc., 1980), pp. 363-366.

2. *Catechism of the Catholic Church* (Ligori, MO: Ligori Publications in assoc. with Libreria Editrice Vaticana, 1994), par. 407.

3. Abraham Lincoln, in *American Quotations,* by Gordon Carruth and Eugene Ehrlich (New York: Wings Books, 1992), pars. 12:67, 12:68.

Part One: *A Heritage Worth Preserving*

Chapter 1: *Land of the Free*

1. *WWI: The Encyclopedia of the War Years 1941-1945,* by Norman Polmar and Thomas B. Allen (New York: Reference & Information Publishing, Random House, 1996), s.v. "Lend-Lease."

2. *Random House Encyclopedia,* electronic edition, s.v. "Declaration of Independence."

3. Ronald H. Bailey and the eds. of Time-Life Books, *World War II: The Home Front U.S.A.* (Alexandria, VA: Time-Life Books, 1977), pp. 90-92.

4. Ibid., p. 146.

5. Evan Thomas, "The Plan and the Man," *Newsweek,* 2 June 1997, p. 36.

6. Jason Sherman, "Golden Vittles," *Armed Forces Journal,* May 1998, p. 20.

7. Max Hastings, *The Korean War* (New York: Touchstone, Simon & Schuster, 1987), p. 130.

8. Allan R. Millett and Peter Maslowski, *For the Common Defense* (New York: The Free Press, Macmillan, 1984), p. 552.

9. Ibid., p. 571.

Chapter 2: *Home of the Brave*

1. Millett and Maslowski, *For the Common Defense,* p. 189.

2. Richard Suskind, *The Battle of Belleau Wood* (Toronto, Ontario: Macmillan in assoc. with Collier-Macmillan Canada, Ltd., 1969), p. 78.

3. William K. Goolirck and Ogden Tanner and the eds. of Time-Life Books, *World War II: The Battle of the Bulge* (Alexandria, VA: Time-Life Books, 1979), p. 188.

4. Hastings, *The Korean War,* pp. 196-197.

5. *The Marines in Vietnam — 1968* (Washington, D.C.: Hist. & Museums Div., Hdqts. U.S. Marine Corps, 1998), p. 419 footnote.

6. "Ambush in Mogadishu," *Frontline,* NC Public TV, 29 September 1998.

Chapter 3: *With Liberty and Justice for All*

1. John F. Kennedy, address to the graduating class of the U.S. Naval Academy, 6 June 1962, in *Dictionary of Military and Naval Quotations,* by Col. Robert Debs Heinl Jr. USMC (Ret.) (Annapolis, MD: U.S. Naval Inst., 1966), p. 140.

Part Two: *How Wars Are Won*

Chapter 4: *One Nation under God*

1. Stanley Karnow and the eds. of Life, *Southeast Asia* (New York: Time-Life Books, 1967), p. 107.

2. Memo for the record from H.J. Poole.

3. Jesus, in *New Testament Bible,* John 14:6.

4. *Catechism of the Catholic Church,* par. 2526.

5. *New Testament Bible,* John 14:17.

6. Howard Fineman, "Under Fire," *Newsweek Magazine,* 31 May 1999, p. 26.

7. James Pilcher, Associated Press, "Gun Industry Fires Back After Lawsuits," *Jacksonville (NC) Daily News,* 5 February 1999, p. 4A.

8. David Wallechinsky, "Are We Still Number One," *Parade Magazine*, 13 April 1997, pp. 4,5.

9. N.C. Menon, "Amnesty Comes Down on U.S.," *The Hindustan Times (New Dehli),* 19 June 1997, p. 14.

10. *Catechism of the Catholic Church,* par. 2316.

11. Ibid., par. 2315.

Chapter 5: *A Closer Look at History*

1. *WWII: The Encyclopedia of the War Years 1941-1945,* Polmar and Allen, s.v. "Cassino."

2. Memo for the record from H.J. Poole.

3. Former Marine Navaho codetalker, in "Japanese Codetalkers," *In Search of History,* Hist. Channel, 30 March 1999.

4. Marine infantryman on Iwo Jima, in *Iwo Jima: Legacy of Valor,* by Bill D. Ross (New York: Vintage Books, Random House, 1986), p. 135.

5. John MacDonald, *Great Battles of the Civil War* (New York: Macmillan U.S.A. in assoc. with Marshall Editions, Ltd., 1992), p. 78.

6. Millett and Maslowski, *For the Common Defense,* p. 189.

7. Linda D. Kozaryn, Armed Forces Press Service, "Belleau Wood: Marines' Shrine," *Leatherneck Magazine,* 9 August 1998, p. 14.

8. George B. Clark, *Their Time in Hell: The 4th Marine Brigade at Belleau Wood* (Pike, NH: The Brass Hat, 1996), pp. 40-66.

9. Goolirck and Tanner, *World War II: The Battle of the Bulge,* pp. 30,31.

10. *The Last Days of World War II,* Hist. Channel, 28 March 1999.

11. Charles B. MacDonald, *A Time for Trumpets* (New York: William Morrow & Co., 1985), pp. 604, 605.

12. Millett and Peter Maslowski, *For the Common Defense,* p. 460.

13. Goolirck and Tanner, *World War II: The Battle of the Bulge,* p. 188.

14. Trevor N. Dupuy, David L. Bongard, and Richard C. Anderson Jr., *Hitler's Last Gamble* (New York: Harper Perennial, Harper Collins Publishers, 1994), p. 333.

15. Ibid., pp. 341, 342.

16. Ibid., pp. 463-477.

17. Ibid., pp. 498, 499.

18. Millett and Maslowski, *For the Common Defense,* p. 453.

19. "An Entirely New War" segment of *Korea — the Unknown War* series (London: Thames TV in assoc. with WGBH Boston, 1990), NC Public TV.

20. Hastings, *The Korean War,* p. 196.

21. "An Entirely New War," *Korea — the Unknown War,* NC Public TV.

22. Maj.Gen. Edwin Simmons USMC (Ret.), in "An Entirely New War" segment of *Korea — the Unknown War* series (London: Thames TV in assoc. with WGBH Boston, 1990), NC Public TV.

23. "Many Roads to War," segment of *Korea — the Unknown War* series (London: Thames TV in assoc. with WGBH Boston, 1990), NC Public TV.

24. Gregory Henderson, U.S. Vice Counsel to Korea 1948-1950, in "Many Roads to War" segment of *Korea — the Unknown War* series (London: Thames TV in assoc. with WGBH Boston, 1990), NC Public TV.

25. "An Arrogant Display of Strength" segment of *Korea — the Unknown War* series (London: Thames TV in assoc. with WGBH Boston, 1990), NC Public TV.

26. Chung Il-Wan, S. Korean Constabulary, in "An Arrogant Display of Strength" segment of *Korea — the Unknown War* series (London: Thames TV in assoc. with WGBH Boston, 1990), NC Public TV.

27. Bert Hardy, photographer for the *Picture Post,* in "There is No Substitute for Victory" segment of *Korea — the Unknown War* series (London: Thames TV in assoc. with WGBH Boston, 1990), NC Public TV.

28. Rt.Hon. George Younger M.P., future British Defense Minister (then member of Argyll & Southern Highlanders), in "An Entirely New War" segment of *Korea — The Unknown War* series (London: Thames TV in assoc. with WGBH Boston, 1990), NC Public TV.

29. *The Marines in Vietnam — 1968*, pp. 418-422.

30. Memo for the record from H.J. Poole.

31. *The Marines in Vietnam — 1968*, p. 419 footnote.

32. Matthew Schott (attributed).

33. Mark Bowden, Staff Writer, "Blackhawk Down," *Philadelphia (Inquirer) On Line,* 16 November 1997, http://www3.phillynews.com/packages/somalia/ncv16/rang16.asp.

Chapter 6: *Were Ideals Followed?*

1. *The Last Days of World War II,* Hist. Channel, 28 March 1999.

2. "Truman," *American Experience,* NC Public TV, 5 October 1997.

3. Keith Wheeler and the eds. of Time-Life Books, *World War II: Bombers over Japan* (Alexandria, VA: Time-Life Books, 1990), pp. 168-170.

4. *The Catholic Encyclopedia,* http://www.knight.org/advent/cathen/09744a.htm, s.v. "Japanese Martyrs."

5. Ibid.

6. Douglas Coe, *The Burma Road* (New York: Julian Messner, 1946), p. 191.

7. Bruce Cumings, in "The Battle of the Minds" segment of *Korea — the Unknown War* series (London: Thames TV in assoc. with WGBH Boston, 1990), NC Public TV.

8. "The Battle of the Minds" segment of *Korea — the Unknown War* series (London: Thames TV in assoc. with WGBH Boston, 1990), NC Public TV.

9. Col. William H. Dabney USMC (Ret.), "The Next Stop Is Saigon," *Marine Corps Gazette,* June 1998, p. 32.

10. "Guerrilla Wars," *Peoples' Century* (London: BBC TV in assoc. with WGBH Boston), NC Public TV, 29 June 1999.

11. David Esler, "The Ho Chi Minh Trail," chapter 26 of *NAM: The Vietnam Experience 1965-75* (London: Orbis Publishing Limited, 1987), p. 130.

12. *Vietnam War Almanac,* gen. ed. John S. Bowman (New York: World Almanac Publications, 1985), p. 358.

13. "Guerrilla Wars," *Peoples' Century,* NC Public TV.

14. Mahatma Gandhi (attributed).

15. "Pope John Paul II: Statement of Faith," *Biography,* A&E Home Video Cat. No. #AAE-10452.

16. Col. David H. Hackworth U.S. Army (Ret.) and Julie Sherman, *About Face* (New York: Simon & Schuster, 1989), p. 594.

17. C.D.B. Bryan, *Friendly Fire* (New York: G.P. Putnam's Sons, 1976), p. 380.

18. *Encyclopedia of the Vietnam War,* ed. Stanley I. Kutler (New York: Charles Scribner's Sons, 1996), s.v. "casualties."

19. Ibid.

Chapter 7: *U.S. Warfare Style in Perspective*

1. Pope John Paul II, *Crossing the Threshold of Hope* (New York: Alfred A. Knopf, 1995), pp. 205, 206.

2. *Catechism of the Catholic Church,* par. 2309.

3. Ibid., par. 2314.

Chapter 8: *The Winds of Change*

1. Col. Joseph H. Alexander USMC (Ret.), "Tarawa: The Ultimate Opposed Landing," *Marine Corps Gazette,* November 1993, p. 57.

2. *When Trumpets Fade* (New York: HBO Home Box Office, a Division of Time Warner Entertainment Co., 1998), filmstrip.

3. *Saving Private Ryan* (Hollywood: Dreamworks and Paramount Pictures, 1998), filmstrip.

4. *TM-E 30-480,* "Handbook on Japanese Military Forces" (Baton Rouge, LA: LSU Press, 1991; reprint Washington, D.C.: U.S. War Dept., 1944), p. 85.

5. *TM-E 30-451,* "Handbook on German Military Forces" (Baton Rouge, LA: LSU Press, 1990; reprint Washington, D.C.: U.S. War Dept., 1945), pp. 210-212.

6. *NVA-VC Small Unit Tactics & Techniques Study, Part I,* U.S.A.R.V., ed. Thomas Pike (Washington, D.C.: Archival Publishing, 1997), pp. II-4, II-5.

7. *TM 30-340,* "Handbook On U.S.S.R. Military Forces" (West Chester, OH: G.F. Nafziger, 1997; reprint Washington, D.C.: U.S. War Dept., 1945), p. V-121.

8. *Platoon* (Hollywood: Hemdale Film Corportion and Orion Pictures, 1986), filmstrip.

9. *The Dirty Dozen* (Hollywood: Metro-Golden Mayer, Inc., 1967), filmstrip.

10. Martin Middlebrook, *The First Day on the Somme* (New York: W.W. Norton & Co., 1972), pp. 189, 190.

11. Charles C. Sharp, "Soviet Infantry Tactics in World War II," from *Soviet Combat Regulations of 1942* (West Chester, OH: George Nafziger, 1998), par. 86.

12. *TM-E 30-480,* "Handbook on Japanese Military Forces," p. 98.

13. *NVA-VC Small Unit Tactics & Techniques Study, Part I,* U.S.A.R.V., ed. Thomas Pike, p. VI-5.

14. Nora Levin, *The Holocaust* (New York: Thomas Y. Crowell Co., 1968), pp. 343-352.

15. Bruce I. Gudmundsson, *Stormtroop Tactics — Innovation in the German Army 1914-1918* (New York: Praeger, 1989), p. 49.

16. *TM-E 30-480,* "Handbook on Japanese Military Forces," pp. 102, 103, 118, 119.

17. *TM-E 30-451,* "Handbook on German Military Forces," pp. 230, 232.

18. *TM 30-340,* "Handbook On U.S.S.R. Military Forces," p. V-47.

19. Nicholas Warr, *Phase Line Green* (New York: Ivy, 1997), pp. 106-158.

Part Two: *For Those Who Still Serve*

Chapter 9: *A Job for the Tactical Technicians*

1. *Random House Encyclopedia,* s.v. "Fredericksburg, Battle of."

2. Middlebrook, *The First Day on the Somme,* pp. 299-302.

3. FMFM 6-4, *Marine Rifle Company / Platoon,* from Marine Corps Develop. & Educ. Cmd. (Washington, D.C.: Hdqts. U.S. Marine Corps, 1978), p. 5.

4. Georgi K. Zhukov, Marshal of the Soviet Union, *Reminiscences and Reflections*, 1974, in *Warriors' Words — A Quotation Book,* by Peter G. Tsouras (London: Cassel Arms & Armour, 1992), p. 282.

Chapter 10: *A Different View of the World*

1. William S. Lind, *Maneuver Warfare Handbook* (Boulder, CO: Westview Press, 1985), pp. 4-8.
2. H.J. Poole, *The Last Hundred Yards: The NCO's Contribution to Warfare* (Emerald Isle, NC: Posterity Press, 1997), p. 350.

Chapter 11: *Preserving Limited Assets in Wartime*

1. Memo for the record from H.J. Poole.
2. Edward J. Drea, Leavenworth Papers No. 2, *Nomanhan: Japanese — Soviet Tactical Combat, 1939* (Fort Leavenworth, KS: Combat Studies Inst., U.S. Army Cmd. & Gen. Staff College, 1981), pp. 18,19.
3. Boeicho boeikenshujo senshishitsu, ed., *Senshi sosho Kantogun (1) Tai So senbi Nomonhan jiken* [Official War Hist. Series: The Kwantung Army, vol. 1, Preparations for the War against the USSR and the Nomonhan Incident] (Tokyo: Asagumo shimbunsha, 1969), p. 36, in Edward J. Drea, Leavenworth Papers No. 2, *Nomanhan: Japanese — Soviet Tactical Combat, 1939* (Fort Leavenworth, KS: Combat Studies Inst., U.S. Army Cmd. & Gen. Staff College, 1981), p. 19.
4. Drea, Leavenworth Papers No. 2, *Nomanhan: Japanese — Soviet Tactical Combat, 1939,* p. 19.
5. Memo for the record from H.J. Poole.
6. Ibid.
7. Ibid.
8. Col. G.C. Thomas USMC, Maj.Gen. Vandegrift's Chief of Staff, in FMFRP 12-110, *Fighting on Guadalcanal* (Washington, D.C.: U.S.A. War Office, 1942), p. 65.
9. "First Offensive: The Marine Campaign for Guadalcanal," by Henry I Shaw, Jr., vol. in *Marines in World War II Commemorative Series* (Washington, D.C.: Hist. & Museums Div., Hdqts. U.S. Marine Corps, 1992), p. 25.
10. Irving Werstein, *Guadalcanal* (New York: Thomas Y. Crowell Co., 1963), p. 96.
11. FMFRP 12-9, *Jungle Warfare* (Quantico, VA: Marine Corps Combat Develop. Cmd., 1989), p. 41.

12. Unidentified NCO's to Chesty Puller, in FMFRP12-110, *Fighting on Guadalcanal* (Washington, D.C.: U.S.A. War Office, 1942), pp. 35-37.

13. Eric Hammel, *Guadalcanal: Starvation Island* (New York: Crown Publishers, 1987), p. 315.

14. Richard Tregaskis, *Guadalcanal Diary* (New York: Landmark Books, an imprint of Random House, 1955), p. 167.

15. Merrill B. Twining, *No Bended Knee* (Novato, CA: Presidio Press, 1996), p. 121.

16. Hammel, *Guadalcanal: Starvation Island,* pp. 318-320.

17. William J. Owens, *Green Hell: The Battle for Guadalcanal* (Central Point, OR: Hellgate Press, a Division of PSI Research, 1999), p. 145.

18. Memo for the record from H.J. Poole.

19. Ibid.

20. Ibid.

21. *NVA-VC Small Unit Tactics & Techniques Study, Part I,* U.S.A.R.V., ed. Thomas Pike, pp. I-3 — I-6.

22. Reg G. Grant, "Fighting the VC Way," chapter 29 of *NAM: The Vietnam Experience 1965-75* (London: Orbis Publishing Limited, 1987), pp. 148-150.

23. Herbert Christian Merillat, *Guadalcanal Remembered* (New York: Donn, Mead & Co., p. 1982), p. 137.

24. *The Guadalcanal Campaign* (Washington, D.C.: Historical Branch, Hdqts. U.S. Marine Corps, 1949; reprint New York: Greenwood Press, 1969), pp. 85, 86.

25. FMFRP 12-34-I, "Pearl Harbor to Guadalcanal," by Lt.Col. Frank O. Hough, Maj. Verle E. Ludwig, and Henry I. Shaw, Jr., vol I. of *History of the U.S. Marine Corps Operations in World War II* series (Quantico, VA: Marine Corps Combat Develop. Cmd., 1989; reprint Washington, D.C.: Historical Branch, Hdqts. U.S. Marine Corps), pp. 303-306.

26. Werstein, *Guadalcanal,* p. 96.

27. Richard B. Frank, *Guadalcanal: The Definitive Account of the Landmark Battle* (New York: Random House, 1990), p. 240.

28. FMFRP 12-34-I, "Pearl Harbor to Guadalcanal," vol I. of *History of the U.S. Marine Corps Operations in World War II* series, p. 308.

29. William H. Bartsch, "Crucial Battle Ignored," *Marine Corps Gazette,* September 1997, pp. 82-84.

30. Phillip D. Birkitt, *Guadalcanal Legacy, 50th Anniversary, 1942-1992* (Paducah, KY: Turner Publishing, 1992), p. 44.

31. Burke Davis, *Marine* (New York: Bantam, 1964), p. 140.

32. FMFRP 12-34-I, "Pearl Harbor to Guadalcanal," vol I. of *History of the U.S. Marine Corps Operations in World War II* series, p. 334.

33. "First Offensive: The Marine Campaign for Guadalcanal," Shaw, p. 38.

34. *The Guadalcanal Campaign,* Hdqts. U.S. Marine Corps, p. 118.

35. Frank, *Guadalcanal,* pp. 356, 357.

36. Davis, *Marine,* pp. 143, 145.

37. Werstein, *Guadalcanal,* p. 149.

38. Birkitt, *Guadalcanal Legacy,* p. 54.

39. Werstein, *Guadalcanal,* p. 150.

40. FMFRP 12-34-I, "Pearl Harbor to Guadalcanal," vol I. of *History of the U.S. Marine Corps Operations in World War II* series, pp. 336, 337.

41. Ibid., p. 328.

42. Gudmundsson, *Stormtroop Tactics,* p. 191.

43. Davis, *Marine,* p. 140.

44. FMFRP12-110, *Fighting on Guadalcanal* (Washington, D.C.: U.S.A. War Office, 1942), p. 2.

45. Gudmundsson, *Stormtroop Tactics,* pp. 147-149.

46. Ibid., p. 21.

47. *Japan / Hong Kong — Singapore,* narrated by John Temple, vol. 1 of "Asian Insights Series" (Lindfield NSW, Australia: Film Australia), distributed by Films Inc. of Chicago, IL, as videocassette 0188-9019.

48. Lind, *Maneuver Warfare Handbook,* p. 25.

49. Sun Tzu, *The Art of War,* trans. and with an introduction by Samuel B. Griffith, foreword by B.H. Liddell Hart (New York: Oxford Univ. Press, 1963), p. 82.

50. Memo for the record from H.J. Poole.

51. Matthew Schott (attributed).

52. John A. Cash, "Battle of Lang Vei," from *Seven Firefights in Vietnam,* by John A. Cash, John Albright, and Allan W. Sandstrum (Washington, D.C.: Center of Military Hist., U.S. Army, 1985), pp. 109-138.

53. Memo for the record from H.J. Poole.

54. *TM-E 30-480,* "Handbook on Japanese Military Forces," p. 117.

Chapter 12: *Doing More with Less in Peacetime*

1. George S. Patton, *War as I Knew It,* 1947, in *A Dictionary of Military Quotations,* by Trevor Royale (New York: Simon & Schuster, 1989), p. 108.

Chapter 13: *An Interim Solution for Units*

1. FMFM 6-4, *Marine Rifle Company / Platoon*, p. 5.
2. Memo for the record from H.J. Poole.

Chapter 14: *The Real Need: Military Reform*

1. Lt.Gen. Arthur S. Collins Jr. U.S. Army (Ret.), *Common Sense Training — A Working Philosophy for Leaders* (Novato, CA: Presidio Press, 1978), p. 214.
2. John A. English, *On Infantry* (New York: Praeger, 1981), p. 217.
3. Lind, *Maneuver Warfare Handbook*, p. 25.
4. Davis, *Marine*, pp. 69,70.
5. "The Battle of the Minds," *Korea — the Unknown War*, NC Public TV.
6. Cumings, "The Battle of the Minds," *Korea — the Unknown War*, NC Public TV.
7. Ibid.
8. *WWII: The Encyclopedia of the War Years 1941-1945*, Polmar and Allen, s.v. "casualties."
9. Member of U.S. Strategic Bombing Survey Team, in *Last Days of World War II*, Hist. Channel, 28 March 1999.
10. "Guerrilla Wars," *Peoples' Century*, NC Public TV.
11. Hackworth and Sherman, *About Face*, p. 818.
12. Ken Butigan, in collaboration with Patricia Bruno, O.P., *From Violence to Wholeness* (Las Vegas: Pace e Bene Franciscan Nonviolence Center, 1997), pp. 2, 3.
13. *Random House Encyclopedia*, electronic edition, s.v. "Declaration of Independence."
14. Field Marshal Erwin Rommel, *The Rommel Papers*, 1953, in *Warriors' Words — A Quotation Book*, by Peter G. Tsouras (London: Cassel Arms & Armour, 1992), p. 224.

Chapter 15: *Decentralizing Control Works*

1. Edmund Burke (attributed).
2. Memo for the record from H.J. Poole.
3. General Vo Nguyen Giap, "Once Again We Will Win," *The Military Art of Peoples' War*, ed. Russel Stetler (New York: Monthly Review Press, 1970), pp. 264, 265.

4. Chesty Puller in *Marine,* by Burke Davis (New York: Bantam, 1964), p. 390.

5. Ibid., p. 325.

6. Edwin P. Hoyt, *The Marine Raiders* (New York: Pocket Books, Simon & Schuster, 1989), p. 16.

7. Terrence Maitland and Peter McInerney, *Vietnam Experience: A Contagion of War* (Boston, MA: Boston Publishing, 1968), p. 97.

8. Gudmundsson, *Stormtroop Tactics — Innovation in the German Army 1914-1918,* pp. 146,147.

9. Timothy T. Lupfer, Leavenworth Papers No. 4, *The Dynamics of Doctrine: The Changes in German Tactical Doctrine during the First World War* (Fort Leavenworth, KS: Combat Studies Inst., U.S. Army Cmd. & Gen. Staff College, 1981), in MCI 7401, *Tactical Fundamentals,* 1st course in Warfighting Skills Program (Washington, D.C.: Marine Corps Inst., 1989), p. 43.

10. Gudmundsson, *Stormtroop Tactics — Innovation in the German Army 1914-1918,* pp. 146,147.

11. Ibid., p. 157.

12. Ibid., pp. 173-175.

13. Ibid., p. 173.

14. *Catholic Almanac: 1998,* Eds. Felicia Foy, O.F.M., and Rose M. Avato (Huntington, IN: Our Sunday Visitor Publishing, 1998), p. 368.

15. "The Dogmatic Constitution of the Church," section 1 from *Vatican II,* in "Laity" of *The Three Days* series (Dallas, TX: National Secretariat of the Cursillo Movement, 1982), p. 7.

16. "Decree of the Apostolate of the Laity," section 7 from *Vatican II,* in "Laity" of *The Three Days* series (Dallas, TX: National Secretariat of the Cursillo Movement, 1982), p. 22.

17. "Light & Shadows: Our Nation 25 Years After Roe v. Wade," A Statement of the National Conference of Catholic Bishops, as authorized by General Secretary Monsignor Dennis M. Schnurr, 12 November 1997.

18. *Catechism of the Catholic Church,* par. 409.

Bibliography

Government Manuals and Historical Studies

FMFRP 12-110. *Fighting on Guadalcanal.* Washington, D.C.:
  U.S.A. War Office, 1942.
"First Offensive: the Marine Campaign for Guadalcanal." Henry I.
  Shaw, Jr. *Marines in World War II Commemorative Series.*
  Washington, D.C.: Hist. & Museums Div., Hdqts. U.S. Marine
  Corps, 1992.
FMFM 6-4, *Marine Rifle Company / Platoon.* Marine Corps
  Develop. & Educ. Cmd. Washington, D.C.: Hdqts. U.S. Marine
  Corps, 1978.
FMFRP 12-9. *Jungle Warfare.* Quantico, VA: Marine Corps
  Combat Develop. Cmd., 1989.
FMFRP 12-34-I. "Pearl Harbor to Guadalcanal." *History of the U.S.
  Marine Corps Operations in World War II.* Vol. I. Lt.Col. Frank
  O. Hough, Maj. Verle E. Ludwig, and Henry I. Shaw, Jr.
  Quantico, VA: Marine Corps Combat Develop. Cmd., 1989; from
  Washington, D.C.: Historical Branch, Hdqts. U.S. Marine
  Corps.
The Guadalcanal Campaign. New York: Greenwood Press, 1969;
  from Washington, D.C.: Historical Branch, Hdqts. U.S. Marine
  Corps, 1949.
Leavenworth Papers No. 2. Edward J. Drea. *Nomanhan:
  Japanese —Soviet Tactical Combat, 1939.* Fort Leavenworth,
  KS: Combat Studies Inst., U.S. Army Cmd. & Gen. Staff
  College, 1981.
Leavenworth Papers No. 4. Timothy T. Lupfer. *The Dynamics of
  Doctrine: The Changes in German Tactical Doctrine during the
  First World War.* Fort Leavenworth, KS: Combat Studies Inst.,
  U.S. Army Cmd. & Gen. Staff College, 1981.
The Marines in Vietnam — 1968. Washington, D.C.: Hist. &
  Museums Div., Hdqts. U.S. Marine Corps, 1998.
NVA-VC Small Unit Tactics & Techniques Study, Part I. U.S.A.R.V.
  Ed. Thomas Pike. Washington, D.C.: Archival Publishing, 1997.

Bibliography

Seven Firefights in Vietnam. John A. Cash, John Albright, and Allan
W. Sandstrum. Washington, D.C.: Center of Military Hist., U.S.
Army, 1985.

TM 30-340. *Handbook On U.S.S.R. Military Forces.* West Chester,
OH: G.F. Nafziger, 1997; from Washington, D.C.: U.S. War
Dept., 1945.

TM-E 30-451. *Handbook on German Military Forces.* Baton Rouge,
LA: LSU Press, 1990; from Washington, D.C.: U.S. War
Dept., 1945.

TM-E 30-480. *Handbook on Japanese Military Forces.* Baton Rouge,
LA: LSU Press, 1991; from Washington, D.C.: U.S. War
Dept., 1944.

Civilian Books, Magazine Articles, and Video/Film Presentations

Alexander, Joseph H. "Tarawa: The Ultimate Opposed Landing."
Marine Corps Gazette, November 1993.

"Ambush in Mogadishu." *Frontline.* Boston: WGBH TV.
NC Public TV, 29 September 1998.

Bailey, Ronald H., and the eds. of Time-Life Books. *World War II:
The Home Front U.S.A.* Alexandria, VA: Time-Life Books,
1977.

Bartsch, William H. "Crucial Battle Ignored." *Marine Corps
Gazette,* September 1997.

Birkitt, Phillip D. *Guadalcanal Legacy, 50th Anniversary,
1942-1992.* Paducah, KY: Turner Publishing, 1992.

Bowden, Mark. "Blackhawk Down." *Philadelphia [Inquirer]
On Line,* 16 November 1997.

Bryan, C. D. B. *Friendly Fire.* New York: G.P. Putnam's Sons, 1976.

Clark, George B. *Their Time in Hell: The 4th Marine Brigade at
Belleau Wood.* Pike, NH: The Brass Hat, 1996.

Coe, Douglas. *The Burma Road.* New York: Julian Messner, 1946.

Collins, Arthur S., Jr. *Common Sense Training — A Working
Philosophy for Leaders.* Novato, CA: Presidio Press, 1978.

Dabney, William H. "The Next Stop Is Saigon." *Marine Corps
Gazette,* June 1998.

Davis, Burke. *Marine.* New York: Bantam, 1964.

The Dirty Dozen. Hollywood: Metro-Golden Mayer, Inc., 1967.
Filmstrip.

Dupuy, Trevor N.; David L. Bongard; and Richard C. Anderson Jr. *Hitler's Last Gamble.* New York: Harper Perennial, Harper Collins Publishers, 1994.

Encyclopedia of the Vietnam War. Ed. Stanley I. Kutler. New York: Charles Scribner's Sons, 1996.

English, John A. *On Infantry.* New York: Praeger, 1981.

Esler, David. "The Ho Chi Minh Trail," chapter 26 of *NAM: The Vietnam Experience 1965-75.* London: Orbis Publishing Ltd., 1987.

Fineman, Howard. "Under Fire." *Newsweek Magazine,* 31 May 1999.

Frank, Richard B. *Guadalcanal: The Definitive Account of the Landmark Battle.* New York: Random House, 1990.

Gardner, Brian. *The Big Push.* New York: William Morrow & Co., 1963.

Giap, General Vo Nguyen. "Once Again We Will Win." *The Military Art of Peoples' War.* Ed. Russel Stetler. New York: Monthly Review Press, 1970.

Goolirck, William K.; Ogden Tanner; and the eds. of Time-Life Books. *World War II: The Battle of the Bulge.* Alexandria, VA: Time-Life Books, 1979.

Grant, Reg G. "Fighting the VC Way," chapter 29, *NAM: The Vietnam Experience 1965-75.* London: Orbis Publishing Ltd., 1987.

Gudmundsson, Bruce I. *Stormtroop Tactics — Innovation in the German Army 1914-1918.* New York: Praeger, 1989.

"Guerrilla Wars." *Peoples' Century.* London: BBC TV in assoc. with WGBH Boston. NC Public TV, 29 June 1999.

Hackworth, David H., and Julie Sherman. *About Face.* New York: Simon & Schuster, 1989.

Hammel, Eric. *Guadalcanal: Starvation Island.* New York: Crown Publishers, 1987.

Hastings, Max. *The Korean War.* New York: Touchstone, Simon & Schuster, 1987.

Hoyt, Edwin P. *The Marine Raiders.* New York: Pocket Books, 1989.

"Japanese Codetalkers." *In Search of History.* Hist. Channel, 30 March 1999.

Karnow, Stanley and the editors of Life. *Southeast Asia.* New York: Time-Life Books, 1967.

Korea — the Unknown War. London: Thames TV in assoc. with WGBH Boston, 1990.

Kozaryn, Linda D. Armed Forces Press Service. "Belleau Wood: Marines' Shrine." *Leatherneck Magazine*, 9 August 1998.

The Last Days of World War II. Hist. Channel, 28 March 1999.

Levin, Nora. *The Holocaust.* New York: Thomas Y. Crowell Co., 1968.

Lind, William S. *Maneuver Warfare Handbook.* Boulder, CO: Westview Press, 1985.

MacDonald, Charles B. *A Time for Trumpets.* New York: William Morrow & Co., 1985.

MacDonald, John. *Great Battles of the Civil War.* New York: Macmillan U.S.A. in assoc. with Marshall Editions, Ltd., 1992.

Maitland, Terrence, and Peter McInerney. *Vietnam Experience: A Contagion of War.* Boston, MA: Boston Publishing, 1968.

Menon, N.C. "Amnesty Comes Down on U.S." *The Hindustan Times (New Dehli),* 19 June 1997.

Merillat, Herbert Christian. *Guadalcanal Remembered.* New York: Donn, Mead & Co., 1982.

Middlebrook, Martin. *The First Day on the Somme.* New York: W.W. Norton & Co., 1972.

Millett, Allan R., and Peter Maslowski. *For the Common Defense.* New York: The Free Press, 1984.

Owens, William J. *Green Hell: The Battle for Guadalcanal.* Central Point, OR: Hellgate Press, a Division of PSI Research, 1999.

Pilcher, James. Associated Press. "Gun Industry Fires Back After Lawsuits." *Jacksonville (NC) Daily News*, 5 February 1999.

Platoon. Hollywood: Hemdale Film Corportion and Orion Pictures, 1986. Filmstrip.

Poole, H.J. *The Last Hundred Yards: The NCO's Contribution to Warfare.* Emerald Isle, NC: Posterity Press, 1997.

Ross, Bill D. *Iwo Jima: Legacy of Valor.* New York: Vintage Books, a Div. of Random House, 1986.

Saving Private Ryan. Hollywood: Dreamworks and Paramount Pictures, 1998. Filmstrip.

Sharp, Charles C. "Soviet Infantry Tactics in World War II," from *Soviet Combat Regulations of 1942.* West Chester, OH: George Nafziger, 1998.

Sherman, Jason. "Golden Vittles." *Armed Forces Journal*, May 1998.

Suskind, Richard. *The Battle of Belleau Wood.* Toronto, Ontario: Macmillan in assoc. with Collier-Macmillan Canada, Ltd., 1969.

Thomas, Evan. "The Plan and the Man." *Newsweek*, 2 June 1997.

Tregaskis, Richard. *Guadalcanal Diary*. New York: Landmark Books, an imprint of Random House, 1955.

True Stories of World War II. Ed. Nancy J. Sparks. Pleasantville, NY: The Readers Digest Assoc., 1980.

"Truman." *The American Experience*. NC Public TV, 5 October 1997.

Twining, Merrill B. *No Bended Knee*. Novato, CA: Presidio Press, 1996.

Vietnam War Almanac. Gen. ed. John S. Bowman. New York: World Almanac Publications, 1985.

Wallechinsky, David. "Are We Still Number One," *Parade Magazine*, 13 April 1997.

Warr, Nicholas. *Phase Line Green*. New York: Ivy, 1997.

Werstein, Irving. *Guadalcanal*. New York: Thomas Y. Crowell Co., 1963.

Wheeler, Keith, and the eds. of Time-Life Books. *World War II: Bombers over Japan*. Alexandria, VA: Time-Life Books, 1990.

When Trumpets Fade. New York: HBO Home Box Office, a Division of Time Warner Entertainment Co., 1998. Filmstrip.

WWII The Encyclopedia of the War Years 1941-1945. Norman Polmar and Thomas B. Allen. New York: Reference & Information Publishing, Random House, 1996.

Religious References

Butigan, Ken, in collaboration with Patricia Bruno, O.P. *From Violence to Wholeness,* Las Vegas: Pace e Bene Franciscan Nonviolence Center, 1997.

Catechism of the Catholic Church. Ligori, MO: Ligori Publications in assoc. with Libreria Editrice Vaticana, 1994.

Catholic Almanac: 1987. Ed. Felicia Foy, O.F.M., Assoc. Ed. Rose M. Avato. Huntington, IN: Our Sunday Visitor Publishing, 1987.

The Catholic Encyclopedia. On-line ed. http://www.knight.org/advent/cathen.

"Decree of the Apostolate of the Laity." *Vatican II Documents*.

"The Dogmatic Constitution of the Church." *Vatican II Documents*.

John Paul II. *Crossing the Threshold of Hope*. New York: Alfred A. Knopf, 1995.

"Light & Shadows: Our Nation 25 Years After Roe v. Wade." A Statement of the National Conference of Catholic Bishops, as authorized by General Secretary Monsignor Dennis M. Schnurr, 12 November 1997.

Bibliography

New Testament Christian Bible.

"Pope John Paul II: Statement of Faith." *Biography.* A&E Home Video Cat. No. #AAE-10452.

About the Author

After almost 28 years as a commissioned or non-commissioned infantry officer, John Poole retired from the United States Marine Corps in April 1993. On active duty, he studied small-unit tactics for nine years: six months at the Basic School in Quantico (1966), seven months as a platoon commander in Vietnam (1966-67), three months as a rifle company commander at Camp Pendleton (1967), five months as a regimental headquarters company commander in Vietnam (1968), eight months as a rifle company commander in Vietnam (1968-69), five and a half years as an instructor with the Advanced Infantry Training Company (AITC) at Camp Lejeune (1986-92), and one year as the SNCOIC of the 3rd Marine Division Combat Squad Leaders Course (CSLC) on Okinawa (1992-93).

While at AITC, he developed, taught, and refined courses of instruction on maneuver warfare, land navigation, fire support coordination, call for fire, adjust fire, close air support, M203 grenade launcher, movement to contact, daylight attack, night attack, infiltration, defense, offensive Military Operations in Urban Terrain (MOUT), defensive MOUT, NBC defense, and leadership. While with CSLC, he further refined the same periods of instruction and developed others on patrolling.

He has completed all of the correspondence school requirements for the Marine Corps Command and Staff College, Naval War College (1000-hour curriculum), and Marine Corps Warfighting Skills Program. He is a graduate of the Camp Lejeune Instructional Management Course, the 2nd Marine Division Skill Leaders in Advanced Marksmanship (SLAM) Course, and the East-Coast School of Infantry Platoon Sergeants' Course.

Since retirement, he has researched small-unit tactics of other nations and written *The Last Hundred Yards: The NCO's Contribution to Warfare* — a squad combat study based on the consensus opinions of 1200 NCO's and the casualty statistics of hundreds of field trials at AITC and CSLC. As of May 1999, he had conducted multiday training sessions for 22 Marine battalions (14 of them infantry) on how to acquire common-sense warfare capabilities at the small-unit level.

Name Index

A

Acheson, Dean 6
Afganistan 105
Aidid, Mohammed Farrah 12, 37
An Hoa 77
Ardennes [Forest] 30, 31
Atlanta 22

B

Banta, Sheffield 73
Basilone, "Manila" John 84
Bastogne 32
Battle of the Bulge 10, 30, 31
Belleau Wood 10, 27, 28, 29
Berlin Airlift 6, 101
Berry 29
Bouresches 29
Briggs 84
Buddha 20, 70
Burke, Edmund 108
Burnside, Ambrose E. 27

C

Calcutta 69
Campbell, Don 56
Carlson, Evans F. 111

Charlie Ridge 35, 36
Chechnya 105
Cheju Island 33, 34
Chicago 21
Chung Il-Wan 34
Cold War 7, 101
Collins, Arthur S., Jr. 100
Cukela 62
Cumings, Bruce 41

D

Da Nang 36, 76
Dean, William 34
Declaration of Independence
    4, 104
"Destroyers for Bases" Deal 4
Dong Ha 71
Dresden 39
Dunkirk 3

E

"Edson's (Bloody) Ridge"
    73, 80, 83
Edson, Merritt A. "Red Mike"
    73, 80, 82, 83
Eisenhower, Dwight D. 31

To: Posterity Press, P.O. Box 5360, Emerald Isle, NC 28594

From: _____

_____

Subject: *The Last Hundred Yards*; request for

1. Send me this large, fully illustrated book.
2. Enclosed is proof of active-duty, reserve, retired, or veteran status in the U.S. military and check/money order for the total:

Price	$19.95
Shipping Charges	2.80
Tax (North Carolina residents only)	1.20
Total	$23.95

3. I understand that delivery could take up to three weeks.

Signature _____

To: Posterity Press, P.O. Box 5360, Emerald Isle, NC 28594

From: _____

_____

_____

Subject: *One More Bridge to Cross*; request for

1. Send me this colorfully bound, fully illustrated book.
2. Enclosed is a check/money order for the total:

Price	$ 9.40
Shipping Charges	1.60
Tax (North Carolina residents only)	.60
Total	$11.60

3. I understand that delivery could take up to three weeks.

Signature _____

One More Bridge to Cross

Lowering the Cost of War

Author
John Poole

Foreword
Bill Lind